Changed and Accepted

Changed AND ACCEPTED

The Story of How
I MET JESUS IN FEDERAL PRISON

Linda Shrock

ISBN (paperback): 979-8-218-06580-5

Front cover design: Josh Aul, Nexlevel Design, LLC, www.nexleveldesign.com
Editor snd interior layout: Kara Starcher, www.mountaincreekbooks.com

31 30 29 28 27 26 25 24 23 22   1 2 3 4 5

Contents

Part 3: Freedom

Introduction

June 21, 2021
Home · Ohio

ALMOST A DECADE HAS PASSED since I was behind bars in the Federal Correctional Institution in Waseca, Minnesota. I was born and raised Amish, and by God's grace, being inside those prison walls, I had the opportunity to change and never be the same again.

I am Linda S. Mullet, daughter of Simon and Susie (Miller) Mullet. I was born in Middlefield, Geauga County, Ohio, and spent most of my childhood there. I have nine brothers and eight sisters, and we all learned to work hard and obey our elders. That obedience led to a bunch of trouble that I wrote about in my first book, *Betrayed and Rejected: The Story behind the Bergholz Amish Hair Cuttings*. That trouble is what landed me and other members of my family in federal prison.

After I published *Betrayed and Rejected*, people started asking questions about my story. The questions weren't accusatory, but rather people just wanted to know more and better understand what happened in Bergholz, Ohio. I realized I may not have explained things the best (thanks to my Amish education), and I may have forgotten to include parts of the story. As I continue with what happened after the hair cuttings, I'll clarify some of those parts.

My goal with sharing my story is two-fold. First, I want people to understand what happened in Bergholz and how one man, my father, controlled a community. And second, I want to share the lessons I learned and how God changed my life. My goal isn't to put down the people who share in my story, but rather I want to raise God up and give him the praise for changing my life as only he could do.

Since I have seventeen siblings plus ten children of my own, my story contains a lot of names. I thought it best to review who the important characters are and how they are related to me before I tell you what happened after I went to prison.

First is my father, Simon Mullet. He was a man who never apologized for anything and who always made excuses or justified why he did something. He was the head of our family and the bishop of the Bergholz Amish. Because he was the leader and had the power to stop the hair cuttings, the judge sentenced him to the most years in prison. He was released early during the height of the COVID-19 pandemic. Prior to the hair cuttings, he continually separated families in our community and ordered many of us adults to spend time living in the chicken coops so we would confess our sins.

Next is Elias, my husband. I met Elias when I was seventeen and we married not long afterward. My father and Elias did not get along, and their dislike of each other caused tension in our marriage and in the community.

At the beginning of our marriage, I had a miscarriage followed by some others. Doctors recommended surgery to fix the problem, and before long, I gave birth to our first son, Dale. Over the years, he was joined by nine other siblings—Mark, Eddie, Dean, Eve, Elias Jr., Stephen, Alexander, Ivan, and Jeremy. One girl and nine boys. I will always be thankful for my older boys who stepped up and helped me in Bergholz even when they didn't understand what was going on. Today, only two of my children, Eddie and Eve, are still Amish.

I have seventeen siblings and I won't confuse you with all their names. For this story, the most important sibling is my sister Winnie and her husband Adam Troyer. If you remember, Adam decided to move to an Amish community in Pennsylvania, but Winnie didn't go with him. Adam wanted to see his girls and my father denied him visitation. The whole situation turned into a big fiasco involving the police and the local sheriff. Years later, I learned the truth about what really happened between Winnie and Adam, and I'll share that as I continue my story.

But first, I will start with the hair cuttings and what happened afterward. The hair cuttings are what landed me in prison, and I think it's important that readers understand what happened and how I was involved. The first chapters review events included in the final chapters of my first book, *Betrayed and Rejected.*

Part 1

Trial

1

The Attacks

ON OCTOBER 4, 2011, A group of twenty-five men and women from our Amish community in Bergholz, Ohio, attended an auction in a nearby county. On the way home from the auction, some of the men asked their driver to stop at Bishop Ruben Hershberger's house.

Bishop Ruben was the bishop who had helped make the final decision that it was okay to take away Lawrence Troyer's six-month ban without further punishment. (Lawrence Troyer was my sister Winnie's father-in-law. My father shunned Lawrence and his family from our community because they were breaking small rules like having a guitar in their home.) After Lawrence and his family moved to another Amish community, over three hundred Amish bishops met and discussed the Troyer's shunning along with others my father had ordered. After those bishops expressed their opinions, Bishop Ruben and a small committee of other bishops decided to erase what my dad did and to fully accept the Troyers and others shunned from Bergholz. Bishop Ruben also supported Sheriff Frank Abrams when he took Adam and Winnie's girls away from Winnie and our community. So, as a way to send the message that the Bergholz community was not happy with his decisions, the men cut Bishop Ruben's hair and beard completely off.

After visiting Bishop Ruben, the men traveled to Bishop Malachi's home in Carrollton, Ohio. They planned to cut off Malachi's beard and hair, but he met them at the door and did not invite them inside. There was a fight in the yard that involved pulling hair out of beards, but no one's hair was cut.

Because the Hershbergers had called 911, the police came to our community and arrested four of the five men who had entered Bishop Ruben's home and cut his beard. The police took the men to jail, but they later returned with one of the men because the driver had incorrectly identified him by name. The police arrested the correct person along with the fifth man. The three men originally arrested spent six days in jail before their arraignment. The jail punishment was supposed to warn the men to never do such a thing again. At the arraignment, my dad vowed that the attacks would not continue, and he paid the $50,000 bond for each man. After their return, everything settled down for a short time.

Jail time and a $50,000 bond seem extreme for cutting someone's beard, but the charges went deeper than that. The actual charges included kidnapping because the men had forcibly restrained the bishops while cutting their beards and hair. Plus, these weren't the first attacks against people outside the Bergholz community.

On September 6, 2011, the Millers decided to hire a driver to take them two hours away to their parents' home in Geauga County. Their parents had briefly lived in Bergholz but moved away because they did not agree with what was going on in the community. And their parents had sided with Adam and the taking of Winnie's girls from Bergholz. After the parents left Bergholz, my dad started telling the Miller children how poorly their parents had raised them. He fed them full of lies to the point that late one night, the six Miller children and their spouses arrived on their parents' doorstep. Leroy, one of the Miller children, sort of hid his face with his hat and knocked on the door. As soon as Mrs. Miller opened the door, Leroy walked in, dragged his dad out of bed, and with the assistance of the other men, shaved his dad's hair and beard off. Then the women grabbed Mrs. Miller and cut her waist-length hair to just below her ears.

Soon after the Miller boys attacked their parents, Leon, who had been living at our house for a while, decided to invite Douglas Wengard, his brother-in-law and old buddy from Ashland, to visit. Leon's plan was to cut Douglas's hair and beard off because, after Douglas had found out that people were being put in coops to confess their sins, he kept calling the sheriff to search for Leon. Leon thought Douglas should not be nosey and should mind his own business because Douglas had never cared or visited during the previous five years.

Douglas and his wife accepted Leon's invitation and came to visit on a Saturday. Leon told me not to serve coffee because he wanted to put a laxative in Douglas's coffee. We figured Douglas should have known he would be attacked, considering all the things that had happened in our community, but he came into the house and sat in a rocking chair like nothing was going on. The rest of us kept looking at each other and smiling because he didn't have a clue what the plan was. I cooked a good dinner, and we all ate. Then Leon asked Douglas if he wanted to see the crops back in the fields. Douglas was willing to go, so I sat with his wife and visited until the men came back. Douglas was shaved clean and unhappy.

After the arrests in October, Elias invited his parents to visit because it had been about five years since we had seen them. Elias wrote a letter inviting them and promising them they would be safe. Then he told me to read the letter so I knew about it. He signed both of our names on the letter even though I begged him not to sign mine because I didn't want to go to prison and leave my children alone. I knew that Elias planned to attack his dad, Martin Shrock, during the visit, and I knew we had been warned not to attack anyone else.

But Elias didn't listen to me because my dad had given him the orders. At this point in life, Elias would have done anything my dad asked because Elias had always been the outcast. He thought, if he listened to my dad, it would help him be accepted by the family.

One November day, Martin and Arlene, Elias's parents, arrived behind Sheriff Frank in his police car with its lights blinking. Sheriff Frank parked and knocked on our door. Elias opened the door, and Sheriff Frank told us that he wanted to make sure Martin and his wife were going to be completely safe while they visited. Knowing plans had already been made, Elias promised Sheriff Frank that everything would be fine and nobody would get hurt.

I cooked supper for Martin and Arlene, but they didn't want to eat because trust had been lost when they were shunned from the Bergholz community. Plus, they were afraid we had poisoned the food. Martin told us that, after Douglas was at our house, he got extremely sick on the way home, so they figured we had poisoned him. (It was only the laxative working.) So, Elias and I ate supper with the kids and visited afterward. Approximately two hours after supper, Martin said it was time for them to go home, and he thanked us for welcoming them and having a nice visit.

Then, Elias said, "I want to ask you one more thing before you leave, Dad. You always taught us as Amish people to stay away from the sheriff and not ask for their protection. Now, you, as our dad, have done that exact thing."

Martin replied that it wasn't him that had called the sheriff. Elias's brother had called for Martin and Arlene to be protected because Elias's brothers did not trust Elias anymore. Unfortunately, Martin's answer wasn't good enough for Elias. He stood up and went over to the drawers where he had hidden the scissors. He got the scissors out and said, "Well, maybe this will teach you a lesson to not call the sheriff." He then grabbed Martin and started cutting his hair.

Martin struggled to get away, but my older boys instantly stood up and helped Elias by holding Martin by the arm. When Martin saw that there was no chance in fighting back, he just stood there and allowed them to finish cutting his hair and beard. When Arlene saw what was going on, she started screaming for help and ran toward the door. Elias ordered me to grab her and not let her outside. Because Arlene put up a huge fight that was more than I could handle alone, Elias told Eve, our daughter, to help me hold her. All of this was part of Elias's plan to get me and the children involved on purpose. After everything was done, we talked a little and they left.

Now we were scared because Sheriff Frank had told us not to cut hair or do anything stupid. As soon as they left, Elias, the children, and I all walked across the field to my dad's house to let him know the order was finished. Dad and all the women had a good laugh about it and thought it was very funny, but I was so scared I was shaking. We had been warned already to not continue with the beard cuttings, so I was sure we would all get arrested.

2

The Aftermath

Nothing happened for a couple of weeks until November 23, 2011. At six o'clock in the morning, our whole house and farm lit up with flashing bright lights. I knew it was Sheriff Frank, and I yelled loudly to wake the others up. Ed Miller and his children and Leon Miller, who were all living at our house, were upstairs sleeping. When I ran upstairs to wake them up, Ed told me to stay away from the front door. We could hear the police banging on the door and yelling for us. When I went back downstairs, Elias was walking toward the door. I yelled for him to come back. He turned around and went into our bedroom where he picked up three-year-old Jeremy and placed him on his lap. Elias and I sat together on our cedar chest with both bedroom doors closed.

We heard the police come inside, and Sheriff Frank opened our bedroom door. He told us he wanted Elias to come out, but Elias refused. Sheriff Frank entered the bedroom and took hold of Elias's arm. After I picked Jeremy up off Elias's lap, Sheriff Frank handcuffed Elias, took him to the kitchen, and made him sit in a chair. Next, Sheriff Frank went upstairs and handcuffed Ed and Leon. The other officers, mostly members of the Federal Bureau of Investigation, ordered the rest of us to follow in a line and sit on the couch so they could see everyone. Before they left, I was told they were going to take the men to Youngstown, Ohio, to meet a judge and they would let us know what was going on later in the day.

After the FBI and police left, I was alone with all my kids (except Mark and Eddie who were staying upstairs at my dad's shop) plus five of Ed Miller's children. At this point, the children were beside themselves because it was early in the morning and they had watched the police arrest their father. Thirteen kids crying and crying. Before long, someone from Dad's house came over and told us that the authorities had taken Dad and my three brothers—Jonas, Larry, and Delbert. We were devastated.

Louisa, Ed's wife, was living with my father and pregnant with his child at the time. She told me she couldn't take care of her own children, they were crybabies, and I was to keep them. I sent a note to her saying that the children were crying so much I didn't know what to do with them. She replied asking me to bring the children to Dad's house. When we arrived, Louisa took her oldest daughter to the washhouse and spanked her hard with a paddle. She told the girl she was to stay at my house and be quiet. The whole situation was terrible, and I couldn't understand how Louisa could be so mean to her own kids. Almost every night,

I sat with the girls in their room upstairs until they fell asleep while my oldest son, Dale, sat with the boys in their room. The children didn't have a dad or mom anymore, and of course, their hearts were broken.

A couple of days after the men were arrested, all of us women went with a van driver to search for the men. We knew they were in Youngstown, but we did not know where. We searched lots of different facilities but didn't find the right one until almost evening. They were at the Community Corrections Association (CCA) holding facilities in Youngstown. Because it was after visiting hours, we were not allowed to visit. The guards told us what hours to come back the next day and we did. After that first visit, we visited every week and took turns going in since there were a lot of us.

I'd later learn that the raid on our community was coordinated by the FBI and county sheriffs. Approximately seventy-five law enforcement officers worked together to simultaneously make the arrests and search five homes and barns for evidence. Because the beard cuttings had taken place in multiple counties, local law enforcement decided to request federal assistance. With the FBI involved, the charges against the men were no longer on the county and state level and would be handled by federal prosecutors. That meant everyone would receive the same punishment rather than one county deciding harsher sentencing for one person and another county giving someone else less of a sentence for the same crime. It also meant witnesses would only have to testify once rather than for each county case.

Oh, how I regretted ever moving to Bergholz, Ohio. Back when Dad got Louisa pregnant, I begged Elias to pack up and move. Elias actually got out the Budget, an Amish newsletter with news from different communities to help the Amish stay connected with each other. He started searching for another Amish community that he thought we could move to. Before we got too far in our search, someone found out about what we were doing, and Dad locked up Elias in the chicken coops once again. (You can read more about what happened with the chicken coops in *Betrayed and Rejected.*)

3

Manipulation

WITH HALF THE MEN IN our community locked up, life became more difficult. My sons Mark and Eddie were staying above my dad's shop, and I went over to talk with them one evening. Mark told me he was struggling and life was almost more than he could handle. He had a hard time accepting what had gone on in my dad's house with the women and everything else. Now, with some of the men sitting in jail, he was struggling even more. When I left for home that night, I was very upset at my dad. He had promised me that, if I let him handle my boys, I would have the best family anyone could ever have. Now, Mark was in a terrible battle with his own life because of my dad and his actions.

The next thing I heard was that Mark left the Amish. My heart broke. I started praying to God again. While walking on the road shortly after Mark left, my daughter Eve and I found a yellow ribbon that said, "God, protect my warrior." That was my prayer.

One day, I went to Lowe's to buy a few things. To my surprise, I met Mark who was shopping with a friend of his. We talked, and he promised to come visit at the house. He didn't show up on the day he said he would, but he did come another day. We talked for some time before he broke the news to me that he didn't want to come back to the Amish. He'd found good people to stay with and they treated him like family. Hearing my son say he was leaving our home and community ripped my heart apart, and I cried and cried.

Later, Mark did come back home to stay. All went well until my dad stuck his nose in my house and business again. Late one night, a few of my sisters came over, woke me up, and said Dad said Mark had to leave or he'd kick my entire family out of the church. Dad gave me two weeks to make the choice. Why was my dad, who was in jail at the time, forcing me to make a decision? Because Mark was telling stories about riding 4-wheelers and Dad was afraid more boys would want to leave the community and have fun with 4-wheelers and trucks.

The decision was hard. I had all my younger children to consider, plus I was under my dad's authority since he was the bishop. In the end, I chose to tell Mark to leave. My choice ripped my heart apart again and crushed it. I wondered if my heart would ever heal. Mark was my child, and I knew there was nothing wrong with him or the things he'd done. He was a good kid.

After Mark left the second time, I found out that he went to live in another Amish community where his uncles, Elias's brothers, lived. I couldn't allow that to happen—Elias's family was an "enemy" of the Bergholz Amish at that point in time. So, I called Mark one night and told him to come home. Mark asked me to promise I wouldn't send him away again, and I made that promise because I thought I was strong enough to stand up for my son. Mark packed up all his things and moved back home. And then my dad found out.

Dad made the same ultimatum again—Mark leaves or my whole family, including me, leaves. If I would've known the future, I would've chosen to keep my children all together and leave the Amish back then. But I didn't know the future nor any Englishers to help me get started in a life away from the only lifestyle I knew.

I broke my promise to Mark. I told him to leave and go live with my brother Brian. I cried and cried. I was confused. I was angry. My dad was determined to break up my family, and I was trying to hang on with all my strength, what little I had left.

Time passed, and Mark decided to come back to the Bergholz Amish again. My mom told him that, if he came back, he had to get rid of his drivers license and car. He gave his car to Brian, and my mom threw Mark's license in the garbage. Mark also wasn't allowed to come home to live. He had to live at my sister Maggie's house.

One day, I was sitting at my table when a hat flew in through the doorway. Mark was standing there and asked if he could come in. I said yes, and we talked for some time. The visit felt good. Just before I was to leave for prison, I sent word to Mark to come home and eat another meal before I left. And then I got scared and was afraid of what my dad would do if he found out. So, the day Mark was supposed to come, I sent a note telling him he better just stay away. I didn't want my dad chasing him out of the community again, especially since our family would need Mark while Elias and I were in prison.

Telling Mark not to come for that visit crushed my heart again. I felt like my life was in pieces. I would've never treated my own children like I did if my dad and others hadn't been behind the scenes forcing me to make choices. My dad's family had been destroyed, and it seemed like he was determined to make sure all the other families were destroyed too. To me, my dad hates beautiful families and beautiful things and he will do what he can to destroy the beauty. One day, my sister Winnie told me to my face that since her family and her life were destroyed, she was going to make sure my life was destroyed as well. If she couldn't have her family, I wouldn't have mine either. I didn't fully understand her because I had nothing to do with her life and it wasn't my fault her family had been destroyed.

My dad has a very bad habit of turning people against each other just by using his words. He separated parents and children and then spoke against the parents to the children so they would agree with him and not their parents. He would tell the church they weren't listening to the rules and then separate families as a punishment. He'd tell someone that another person said something against them, even if that person never did. Dad was manipulative and corrupted people's minds against each other.

The best example of Dad using his words to manipulate is Adam and Winnie's story. He started accusing Adam of sleeping with his own mother, even though Adam insisted it wasn't true. Dad made Adam write down the story about his mother and admit to it. I remember hearing Dad say, "Even if it's not true, just write it and see what happens." Dad wanted a reason to separate Adam and Winnie, and the made-up story about Adam would give him that reason. Adam was desperate to have his wife back, so he allowed my dad to convince him to write the story. What happened with Adam's story was the first lie I heard my dad say, but it was sadly only the beginning of the lies and manipulation.

After Adam moved to Pennsylvania, the court ordered that Winnie was allowed to have the girls on the weekends and Adam would have them through the week. One of the court's stipulations was Winnie could have the girls only if she was away from my dad's house and Bergholz because of the things happening there (this was before the hair and beard-cutting attacks). The court said Bergholz was a bad environment with bad influences. The court also banned my dad and three brothers from seeing the girls and said it was for the girls' safety.

The court gave Winnie a location in Pennsylvania where the girls could visit with her, and she'd take a van full of church women with her each time. My dad convinced Winnie it was okay for him to ride along to see the girls. He always hid under pillows in the back of the van so no one would see him violating the court order. He sat in the very back flirting with the church women who took turns going along to support Winnie. Mom rarely had the chance to go along to visit her grandchildren, and I had the opportunity only two times. One day, an Amish man drove by the location in Pennsylvania and saw my dad there. Someone told Adam that Dad wasn't obeying the court order. The courts then banned Dad even harder and pressured Winnie for not abiding by the court order and told her she could lose visitation altogether. Even back then, my dad thought he was above the law.

—4—

The Trial

DURING MARK'S TIME OF COMING and going from the community, those of us who hadn't been arrested received our indictments or notices that it was believed we had committed crimes. All together, sixteen of us—ten men and six women—were arrested or indicted. We faced a combined ninety felony charges that included federal hate crimes, conspiracy, and obstructing justice charges (concealing or destroying evidence). Considering the lengthy list of charges against us, we all needed lawyers to fight our cases. Dad had to pay his lawyer, but the rest of us received lawyers from the court system.

Because most of our families had young children, the judge released me and the other women who were indicted to stay home on bond until our trials were over rather than immediately send us to jail like the men. While home, we were to get things ready and arrange for who would take care of the children during the trial and during any sentencing we received. Each family involved had an adult left to take care of the children if the dad or mom was sent to federal prison. Except for my family. Both Elias and I were facing time in prison. Our ten children were old enough—the youngest was three years old and the oldest was twenty years old—to help take care of each other, but it was still hard thinking about my kids left without parents.

Weeks after our indictments, all of us plus our individual lawyers attended federal court in Cleveland, Ohio, and stood in front of a judge. He gave us each a choice of going to trial before a jury or accepting twenty-five years to life in federal prison without a trial. None of us had the chance to ask Dad what to say because the judge's offer was unexpected. Talk about being scared. I was shaking so badly. All I could think was that I'd be locked up and never able to see my children again if I chose the twenty-five years to life. Without knowing what the others chose, I chose the trial and so did everyone else. If you look at my photo on the back of my first book, *Betrayed and Rejected*, you can see just how scared I was. Even with a trial, I was facing prison life within federal facilities. I was terrified.

On August 28, 2012, our trial began and lasted for three weeks. We were in court every single day. All sixteen of us and our lawyers sat around four tables in the same room at the Cleveland courthouse. The men from the CCA sat at a different table from the rest of us. Their table had covers hanging to the floor so the jury couldn't see who had shackles on their legs and who didn't.

Each morning we all walked into the room single file and

found our seats beside our lawyers. On the first trial day, my lawyer couldn't be there, so one of the other lawyers covered for me.

Approximately twenty-four witnesses testified against us, and the outlook was not looking good at all. My dad decided to not fight back and not testify. Because he wouldn't testify, the rest of us knew we would not be questioned either. He made sure we all knew that he wasn't going to give any of us an opportunity to talk.

The main reason Dad decided to not testify is he knew, if he were to go on the stand, he could not answer the questions without lying. He told us, "Jesus was also quiet at times and didn't say anything." In my mind, I knew the difference—Jesus's accusers were lying about him, and Dad's accusers were speaking the truth. If Dad spoke, he would have to lie—a big difference compared to Jesus being quiet. But if I had spoken my mind and pointed out the difference, I would have received punishment beyond measure. Why? Because Dad said he's one of God's chosen men and nobody speaks against him without punishment. So, I kept my thoughts to myself.

My dad, who never laid a hand on anyone or cut anyone's hair or beard, was arrested with the rest of us because he was the leader in Bergholz. He gave out all the rules and ordered what he wanted everyone to do to others. Nothing happened without him knowing about it or ordering someone to do it. In fact, multiple times during the trial the prosecutors called him the mastermind of the attacks. Whenever the men sat in the circle to visit on Sunday, Wednesday, and Friday nights, Dad gave out orders for what he wanted everyone to accomplish. Then he'd join the women's circle and give the same orders. After the orders were given out to everyone, Dad would roll his chair out of the circle and say, "I want you to know I haven't told you to do anything. If you do this, it will be completely of your own free will."

From a young age, the Amish are taught to obey and respect their elders. This is why the men and women always did their very best to say it was them and that my dad had nothing to do with whatever had happened. My dad was "innocent," but only by our choice to take the blame. And it was Elias's choice to obey my dad and not stand up against him even though he knew it was wrong to attack his own parents.

Two of my sons, Dale and Mark, testified on the stand during the trial. Dale spoke the truth about the camera with the photographic evidence of the hair cuttings. He told how my dad had ordered the men to buy a cheap camera from a dollar store and take before, during, and after photos of the attacks. My dad, who was too chicken to go along for the actual hair cuttings, wanted to see what took place. Remember, to an Amish person, having a photo taken, and especially one that shows the face, means the person now has a graven image before God. They also believe that a photo takes away part of who you are. Taking the before and after photos was meant to humiliate the person, too.

Dale told how Ed Miller, who had been in charge of taking the photos, had been living with us at the time of the hair cuttings. He also said the camera was hidden in our home until my dad realized prosecutors were looking for the camera. Dad had Louisa send me a note to tell Dale to retrieve the camera and give it to his cousin. Dale found the camera hidden in a drawer and gave it to his cousin who, in an attempt to get rid of evidence, stuck the camera in some plastic bags and hid it under a pile of leaves in the woods. On the evening of Dale's court testimony, my dad sent word home that Dale was shunned from everything once again. Dale was allowed to remain in the community, but he could not be with any of us or go with the young folks anywhere because he had told about the camera. However, by the time of the trial and Dale's testimony, the prosecutors had already found the camera, developed the photos, and used them as evidence during the trial.

Not long before the hair cuttings, Dale had been kicked out of the youngie group and was not allowed back in. My sister Lucille didn't have a ride to and from the Sunday night gatherings, so Dale would give her a ride. They had grown up together as kids, and Dale had always been a kind-natured boy who would do anything to make sure Lucille was safe. Sometimes during their conversations, he would put his hand on her leg without thinking about what he was doing. It was his way of reassuring her or letting her know he was listening or understood her. Well, one weekend, all the youngie group, including Dale and Lucille, went to the cabins. Right afterward, Dale was kicked out of the group (no one gave a reason), and he was not allowed back in. That meant that whenever we gathered at my dad's house on Sundays, Wednesdays, and Fridays, Dale had to stay home alone.

It ripped my heart out to see Dale punished like that, especially since there was nothing else for him to do in the community. I knew if I stuck up for him, I would be punished too. But I couldn't help myself, and I asked Lucille why Dale couldn't be part of the group anymore. She said it was because she was having feelings for him and she knew it was wrong. She told our dad about the situation and her feelings and how Dale sometimes put his hand on her leg. My dad twisted the story and blamed Dale for having a dirty mind. He claimed Dale was purposely trying to get Lucille to have feelings. Of course, Dad didn't want to kick his own daughter out, so he kicked Dale out instead.

I didn't tell Dale why he was thrown out until much later when I knew it wouldn't affect him anymore. Maybe I should've told him sooner, but I didn't want him fighting the same battle I did of trying to not hate others for their actions. I knew Dale was a good person and didn't deserve that type of treatment. Then, after he testified, he was told to not have contact with any of the young folk or his family members. Talk about heartbreak.

Verdict

AFTER THREE WEEKS OF TESTIMONY, the twelve-person jury entered deliberations to decide our fate. The jury was responsible for determining whether each individual was guilty of the charges against them. All sixteen of us were charged with conspiracy or agreeing with others to plan and commit a crime. Then each person was charged with the attacks they participated in. I had two charges against me—conspiracy and the attack on Elias's parents because I had grabbed Arlene, Elias's mother, and held her back. Elias had the same charges plus the attack on Douglas Wengard. My dad was charged with nine of the ten different counts. His charges included conspiracy, the five attacks, hiding the camera, and the additional charges of lying to the FBI and directing the men to destroy a bag of hair that they had brought back from one of the attacks.

The jury was also responsible for deciding whether the federal hate crime charges applied. If they found us guilty of hate crimes, the sentencing times would be longer. The prosecutors argued that the attacks were motivated by religion and caused injury or disfigurement—the definition of a religious hate crime. Our lawyers argued that the attacks were motivated by family feuds and disagreements, not religion, and that cutting someone's hair did not cause a disfigurement because hair grew back. They didn't deny that we participated in the attacks or that we had possibly committed crimes. Their point was the attacks didn't fit the definition of a hate crime.

Now, after three weeks of witnesses and testimonies, our fate was in the hands of the jury. The jury deliberated for four-and-a-half days. While we waited on our verdict, a television played in our waiting room. We were Amish and not supposed to watch television, but Mervin decided to switch the channel to a western movie. In my mind at the time, we had been trying to tell the world we weren't violent people, but when Mervin changed the channel to a western movie with shooting and we all sat there watching, we told the world exactly who we were.

Within five minutes of Mervin changing the channel, the verdict was in.

Guilty.

All of us were heading to federal prison.

The jury returned their verdict on September 20, 2012, and we went back to the courthouse on February 8, 2013, for our sentencing. The lengths of our sixteen sentences varied because not everyone had the same charges against them. I received two years while the five other women received one year. My sentence was longer because I was present for two different incidents in my house. Even though I had nothing to do with the attack on Leon's brother-in-law, I received extra time in jail for conspiracy because I was there. Dad received fifteen years, Elias received five years, and the other men received anywhere from three to seven years. The judge said Dad received the longest sentence because he was the leader and he had the authority to stop us but didn't. Dad and two other men were given credit for time already served while waiting for the trial and sentencing.

I'm not sure who had the say with where we were sent to serve our time, but they scattered us all over the country. Most of us were a thousand miles apart in different federal prisons. Dad was sent to Texas, and Elias went to Mississippi. Amelia and I were sent to Waseca, Minnesota. The others went to prisons in Connecticut, Illinois, Louisiana, Massachusetts, Ohio, and West Virginia.

Many times I thought God had left me alone in the wilderness during the years leading up to the attacks and all through the trial and sentencing. But he didn't. He knew how things were going to go and how they would turn out. I don't know what would have happened if I hadn't had God with me the whole time.

Part Two

Prison Life

6

The Trip

ON APRIL 11, 2013, MY lawyer drove me, Amelia, her husband, and my son Eddie to the Cleveland airport. Without my lawyer, we wouldn't have known where to go or even how to check in for our flight. With his help, we boarded our plane headed to Minnesota. The five-hour airplane ride was fun—if I blocked out where I was going. When we arrived in Minnesota, we had two hotel rooms waiting for us for the night. Amelia and I had to check in at the prison at eight o'clock the next morning.

Not knowing what to do that evening, the four of us walked up the road to the Cabella's store. We walked around for a few hours, and the men spent some money playing the hunting games where you use a gun to kill deer, moose, and bears.

When we returned to our rooms, the first thing Eddie did was turn on the television. We could hear through the wall that Amelia and her husband had their television on too. It felt weird listening to something that was forbidden in the Amish culture. But we had done so many things already now that we were not supposed to do that it took the edge off being scared. And I knew that in prison I would have to do a lot of things that were "wrong" for us.

The best part about the hotel room was the shower. For the first time in my life, I was able to take a shower. We always bathed in tubs with the water heated in a big kettle and dumped into the tub. Then cold water is added until the temperature is right. To experience a shower after over thirty years of baths is indescribable. The shower was amazing and felt so good.

That night, I fought anger toward my dad for getting us involved in such a mess. I knew that as soon as I entered the doors to prison, I would be completely separated from all my children. My kids were, and still are, my strength and courage. Dad knew that, if he separated me from my children, I would get weaker. He assumed he would be able to manipulate me better, but that didn't work for him. Now, here I was, ready to enter prison over eight hundred miles away from home, and all because I had listened to my dad's orders. I didn't think I could ever forgive him.

The next morning, the men went with us to the prison where Amelia and I said goodbye to them and entered the federal facility. The men flew home later that day on a plane bigger than the one from the day before.

Sadly, there was no backing out allowed for Amelia and me. All sixteen of us had filed appeals, and I had filed a request to remain home with my children, but I was denied. Now I was entering a federal prison that would become my home for almost two years.

7

Prison

THE PRISON STAFF ORDERED AMELIA and me through the intake process. First, they sent us to a room and told us to change into prison clothes. Wearing a shirt and pants felt very different than wearing a dress. We were told to let down our hair, which felt as strange as wearing pants. A staff member gathered all our hairpins, bobby pins, and elastic bands. Those items went into a bag along with our clothes, shoes, and underwear. Then someone took a photo for our nametags, required to be worn on our clothes at all times. We went to another room where we were registered and received TB vaccinations. At one point during the process, they locked us in separate rooms and served us a lunch of a peanut butter sandwich and an apple. I thought, *Oh boy, here we go.*

Finally, a staff person came and escorted us to Unit C. (The prison complex has different units to house approximately seven hundred inmates.) Oh my, I was shaking so badly. We walked to our unit that had open cells and ten bunk beds in one area to house twenty ladies. The ladies were kind to us and put Amelia and me right beside each other on the top bunks. We had to climb a ladder to get to our bunk, another thing that felt strange.

Assigned to the bottom bed of my bunk was a Black lady. I had been taught that Black people are bad and we were to stay away from them because they can get very angry. I was terrified that first night and didn't sleep well at all. The next morning, I woke up and my bunkie, what we called the person who shared the top or bottom of a bunk, was making coffee. She looked at me, smiled the sweetest smile I'd ever seen in my life, and asked if I wanted some coffee. I told her yes, and she handed me a cup. The coffee was delicious. I was a black coffee drinker, and my bunkie had added other things to the coffee to make it taste wonderful. Somewhere between her sweet smile and the taste of the coffee, all fear left me about Black people. She, along with many other ladies, was so kind to me.

In my mind, I thought the prison ladies were going to beat me up and throw me in a dark cell because the Bergholz Amish claimed I was full of sins and a bad person. I had disagreed with the bishop, my dad, and I should go to hell, according to the Amish. Those thoughts, combined with what I'd been taught about Black people, had me scared about what would happen in prison. But I had a surprise coming my way—the ladies liked me very much and kept telling me I was a great person. Their words confused me and troubled my mind. Why would they say that? If I was supposed to be a sinful person, what did they see that was different?

A photo of me taken during my time in prison. I'm wearing the prison-issued dress and our makeshift head covering.

Sometime during our first week in prison, Amelia and I were escorted to the laundry room where we received dresses with shoulder straps. Putting a dress on after wearing pants felt normal. But even wearing a dress, I still felt naked because I didn't have my head covering.

Not long after we started wearing the dresses, one of the prison pastors sent word that he wanted to see us in the chapel. Amelia and I went, and he started talking about our religion. He didn't understand the Amish ways and tried to get us to wear a Jewish head covering. We both refused.

The commissary, the store inside the prison, had white handkerchiefs, so Amelia and I bought those and started wearing them as our head covering. Unfortunately, wearing the handkerchiefs caused a lot of drama because the handkerchiefs weren't meant to be a sacred head covering. The pastor made us put them away and stop wearing them, but others in the prison fought for us and we were allowed to wear them again. Now, I felt the tension around me. I didn't want something like this to happen at all. I just wanted to live my life the best I could in prison and get out again.

We were allowed to write letters home, but we had to go through a lot of paperwork to be approved to write to other prisons where our family members were. After some time, I was permitted to write back and forth with Elias. The prison also gave us minutes to use to call home. In order to make a call, we had to connect through a computer system that recognized our voice saying our name. I was terrified to make calls because we had been taught to stay away from electronic devices. But if I wanted to talk to my children, I had no choice. Using the computer system was frustrating. If you didn't repeat your name with the exact voice you set it up with, there was no way your call was going through. Sometimes I had to repeat my name three or four times before I got it right.

Amelia had a terrible time making calls too. Many nights she ended up crying because she couldn't say her name right and missed calling home. She knew her family was waiting by the phone for the call too because they had sent a letter stating which nights and times she was supposed to call. Finally, she went to the office and recorded her name again to see if it would work better. Sometimes she got it to work and other times she didn't. One night, she told me she got into a fight over the phone with her husband and she told him not to talk to her again. She didn't say what they fought over, and I didn't ask.

I felt like I was responsible for Amelia, since I was the oldest with more life experience. Plus, I had been one of the women leaders in Bergholz before my dad stripped that from me. As a leader, I knew a bit about Amelia, but not a lot. My strongest memory of her was how angry she got when we took her to my sister Maggie's house instead of my dad's house when we separated her and her husband. After spending more time with her in prison, I realized that all the times she was crying about not calling home weren't because she was afraid or sad that she missed a call. No, it was because she was angry. She also frequently told me she didn't need my help. At all.

The prison staff made it clear to us that we could not just lay in our beds and feel sorry for ourselves. We had to get up by eight o'clock, fix our beds, and get dressed. We would be assigned jobs within the prison, and we had to be physically active. We could go to the gym for exercise. We could walk or run on the two-mile track around the area where other prisoners played games. And we could also sign up for baseball, volleyball, and other team games.

During our first weeks in prison, Amelia and I did everything together, no matter what it was. We decided to sign up for baseball. But the night we planned to sign up, Amelia went without me. She had the day off work and signed up while I was still working rather than waiting for me. I felt left behind and got upset over it. She knew I wanted to go with her but went by herself. I signed up later on, but because she had signed up earlier, she was allowed to start playing on the teams before me. Unfortunately, I let the situation cause some tension between us.

Amelia and I were in prison for about two weeks before we were assigned our first jobs. The kitchen supervisor stopped me in the hallway to the cafeteria and asked if I would help in the kitchen. She found out Amelia and I were Amish and knew we would work. Plus, the kitchen needed help. I told her I would take the job. The supervisor was a staff member, not a prisoner, and she had a feisty attitude with strong willpower. She was short and skinny and super nice. I really liked her. The kitchen was always busy, but she made it fun to work there.

We had time to sit down and chat about our lives from noon until dinner prep began. During our chats, some ladies shared why they were locked up, and others didn't. A lot of the ladies were charged with conspiracy, the same as me. One lady told me she used a shovel on her man because he was drinking. Another lady was dealing drugs for money to support her children and couldn't make the last payment. She ended up tied to a kitchen chair and had the side of her face and the inside of her thighs cut with knives. The police found her before she died and kept her alive. On others, I saw broken noses healed crookedly, so I knew they'd been in fights. I thought about my life. It was nothing compared to what some of the prison ladies had been through.

Amelia and I started working as line servers. The menu every day included rice and beans, salad, etc., on a self-serve salad bar. The meat, like chicken, steak, and meatloaf, and the main vegetables, like sweet potatoes, were served cafeteria-style because each person got only one piece. If we wanted, we could trade our food with someone else if we didn't want it or didn't like it. Taking food from the cafeteria wasn't allowed, but some ladies stuffed food in their clothes and took it to their cells to cook with later. They'd mix it with food they bought at the commissary. They used an iron to heat the food, which worked just fine. The food the ladies cooked without a stove or a microwave amazed me. They were very creative. And several times the staff locked down the prison for an alcohol search. The ladies would take fruit and a few things from the kitchen and make the alcohol in their cells. I could tell the ladies had too much time on their hands and were bored. They did all kinds of things in secret. Sometimes they were caught, and sometimes they weren't.

Every so often, the staff in the hallway randomly picked a couple of ladies and patted them down to see if they hid food in their clothes. Of course, if caught, there was punishment. I never tried sneaking food from the cafeteria. I tried my best to be on good behavior because I hated punishments. I'd been punished so much by my dad, and I was finally a thousand miles away from him and free from his punishments. I didn't want to be punished anywhere else.

Amelia and I had worked in the kitchen for about a month when my supervisor stopped me in the hallway again. She asked if I would mind being a leader in the kitchen on my leader's days off and also stepping up and helping my leader on the other days. I agreed. She told me she planned to make Amelia a leader too because we were both good workers and our days off were different. All went well with our new positions for a bit until Amelia tried to make me look bad.

Amelia told the staff cook that our leader said no one except for her was allowed to make the trays for the ladies in the SHU, what we called solitary confinement. The cook didn't have any reason to doubt Amelia, so he believed her. Amelia came to me and said the lead cook told her no one could make the trays but her. I knew our leader wouldn't have said anything like that, because it meant on Amelia's day off, I wouldn't be allowed to do the trays. I went to our leader and asked if what Amelia said was true. Our leader said she didn't say anything like that. So, I went to the lead cook and told him Amelia lied to him. He was disappointed in her and made her back off from his area.

All I wanted was to stay positive, be free of the drama, and go home to my children again.

8

Friends

A THOUGHT CROSSED MY MIND one day—my siblings back home could do whatever they wanted to my children and tell them anything they wanted, and I could do nothing about it. I was too far away. Some of my siblings never liked me, so they never liked my children either. And I knew just how mean some of my siblings could be. Every day I fought the fear of what my brothers and sisters were doing to my kids without me there to protect them.

Having Amelia with me helped, but we had our share of misunderstandings. And sometimes, she tried her best to cause trouble for me. Before we had left for prison, I had a nervous breakdown. Amelia told me she was afraid with all the things going on in my life that I might have one again. She worried she wouldn't know what to do with me if one did happen. I explained I was hundreds of miles away from my family members now and one wouldn't happen. I felt like she wanted me to have another one so maybe she would get more attention. I never understood why she kept after me about having one. I just wanted to go home again and be with my kids.

Amelia and I both made a lot of new friends, and the differences in who we friended were interesting to me. I wasn't bothered by us having different friends, but I can't say the same for Amelia. Not long after we arrived in prison, another woman came in, and she connected with me instantly. This new woman and I talked a lot. She had a beautiful, outgoing personality. She grew up close to an Amish community and knew about our way of living. She liked Amelia too, but somehow Amelia felt pushed away. I told Amelia that I believed God sent this woman to our prison so I'd have someone with me and not feel so alone when Amelia's time was up. Amelia told me she agreed and felt like this woman was God-sent. Unfortunately, our friendship would cause a lot of issues later on.

Five days after we arrived in prison, I encountered a lieutenant, one of our guards. I was walking to the office to get my mail when this lieutenant walked straight toward me. He yelled that it was time for tornado warning training and everyone was to leave their cells and sit in the hallway until he gave permission to get up. Somehow, I knew God sent this man to help me and show me the way in prison. By the time I'd arrived at the prison, I felt like my whole life had been crushed into tiny pieces. For the first five days, I kept my head up the best I knew how and watched for a sign from God. On day five, when I saw the lieutenant, I knew. I sensed God himself came into the room to help ease my pains and heal my broken heart. I was thrilled and didn't feel so alone anymore. The lieutenant was a nice-looking guy, but I wasn't attracted to him. I only saw the light of God in him.

One night at dinnertime, the lieutenant walked into the cafeteria. His actions drew my attention, and nobody would have guessed he knew I was watching him. God gave me the gift of reading people by their actions, and I often sat quietly watching and learning.

I met so many other beautiful people in prison. We'd sit and talk before bedtime about why the Amish got locked up and how the Amish raise their children and the work involved. I loved to listen to the other ladies tell their life stories because they actually weren't that much different from mine. They dressed differently, had electricity, and drove trucks and cars instead of a horse and buggy. Otherwise, we pretty much had the same life. At night, when I got ready for bed, I let my hair down, changed into nightclothes, and lay in my bunk. Nobody would have guessed I was Amish! I was amazed by how much I was like the other ladies. The Amish teach that worldly people are evil and wrong and are going to hell. Yet, somehow I just knew the prison ladies were good people and the evil people were the Amish. There were bad people in prison, but the good outnumbered the bad.

Over seven hundred inmates were in our facility from different states and also different nationalities. I saw fights, ugly fights like I had never seen before. But if ladies fought, it was because one lady lied or cheated another lady. Not once was there a fight about the different religions or beliefs of the ladies. Most everyone respected the way others dressed without judging. I was impressed because Amish people are judgmental about how others believe or dress. The Amish have a way of looking down on others and they don't think they are judging, but they are.

Many nights when I couldn't sleep, I lay in my bunk thinking. Every four or five hours, staff members would walk around the beds counting to make sure everyone was still there. The rattle of the keys hanging on the staff belts made me cringe and reminded me I was locked up behind steel doors with no way out and no chance of seeing my children anytime soon.

9

Stephen & Mark

ONE DAY, NOT LONG AFTER my prison sentence started, my children called. They said my son Stephen had been admitted to the hospital with severe stomach pains. Before all the hair cutting incidents happened, he'd have stomach pains, but we assumed they were growing pains. Sometimes he would go out to our yard and just lay there for a bit. Then he would get better until the next time.

When Stephen started complaining again, my son Eddie took him to the doctor's office for help. The doctor told Eddie that Stephen had to go to the hospital by ambulance and asked which hospital Eddie preferred. Poor Eddie had to make that decision on his own because he didn't have time to call Elias or me. My heart ached for my children. But I knew there was nothing for me to do except pray and ask God to keep his hand over them.

Stephen's diagnosis ended up way worse than growing pains or what anyone thought. He was admitted to the children's hospital in Pittsburgh where he was diagnosed with a liver disease. The doctor called Elias in prison and had him sign up for insurance because there was no way we could afford a hospital bill. (I thought that was very nice of the doctor, and it made me feel more comfortable.) The doctor talked to Elias, explaining what Stephen's problem was and what the next steps would look like. The children repeated those things to me when they updated me on how things were going. I'd tell the prison ladies what was going on whenever something new happened and they supported me a lot.

The doctors did not understand how Stephen's disease had started. From my perspective, I thought maybe the stress was too much for him and it landed in the weakness of his body. Stephen was one of those children who took things more seriously and let things bother him a lot. He had just lost both parents to prison life, and then he had a puppy, no bigger than a cat, that he was attached to run out and get killed by a driver. That broke Stephen's heart. But no matter where the disease came from, the doctor ordered medicine and IVs.

Long story short, Stephen's disease required chemotherapy treatment, and he lost all his hair. Thankfully, over time, it looked like the chemotherapy was helping him.

At the beginning of the ordeal, Eddie, along with a community member, stayed with Stephen in the hospital. The community members took turns staying. The rest of my children continued with their new normal at home. Then my mom started staying at the hospital with Stephen so the boys could go home, work, and

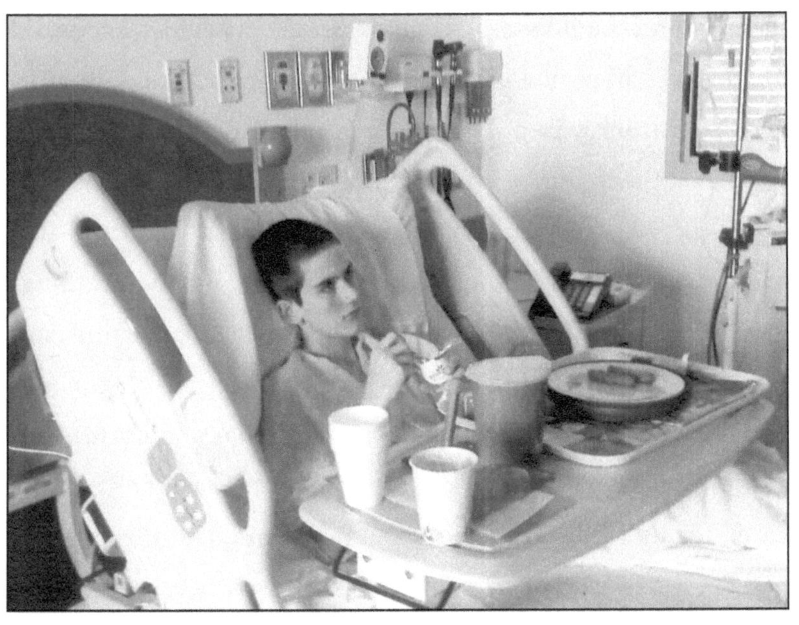

Stephen during his stay in the hospital.

bring in an income. I appreciated my mom staying with Stephen. Mom and I were not on the same page and disagreed many times, but I was thankful she wanted to help with my children.

I fought a lot of anger issues again toward my dad because my prison life was his fault and I was separated from my children when they needed me the most. Every time I thought I was done fighting anger, it popped back up again. Dad wanted revenge on others for things that had happened in the past and he would say the law couldn't stop us. We were doing God's work and God would protect us. His words failed us all and now we were locked up. I think at times Dad felt bad about us parents being away from all our children simply because we had listened to him, but he would make all kinds of excuses about why things happened. My guess is he wanted to push the thought and the guilt away. And even from prison, Dad still controlled Bergholz and what happened there.

Mark, who had returned home to help with the farm while Elias and I were in prison, told me over the phone that things were going great. We had a $30,000 mortgage loan against our house, and Mark said he and his brothers were making money and trying hard to pay off that debt before Elias and I came back home. (It made me feel good that the boys picked up the slack and cared for us while we were locked up.) Mark said they already had $6,000 in the checkbook. I was surprised because that was more money than Elias ever had. To this day, the children and I cannot figure out what Elias was doing with our money because we know the amount he was making and we never had more than $2500–$3000 cleared in the checkbook. Elias even had the boys working with him before he was locked up, and he still never had more money in the checkbook. What was he doing with all that money? I didn't have any. I didn't even have the checkbook. The only time I wrote a check was when I paid the monthly bill at my mom's bulk food store.

Well, not long after Mark told me the amount of money they were making and that things were going great, the drama started. My dad pulled Eddie off the crew and turned him against all his brothers and his cousins. I guess Eddie was going behind the boys' backs and telling my dad what was going on at work. I know Dad ordered Eddie to tell him so he would know what was hap-

Three of my boys who left the Amish before I did. Two left while Stephen was in the hopsital, and the third left a short time after they did.

pening and could control the boys. Dad knew Eddie would listen to him too.

Then Mark and Dean were chased out of the house and told to take their belongings and go live with my sister Maggie again. Mark decided he'd had enough and decided to leave the Amish again, but this time Dean planned to go with him. One day while Mark and Dean were at work, Dad ordered Eddie to pack up Mark's and Dean's belongings and boot them out of the family— and Dad never told Elias or me what was going on! Now I lost two family members because of my dad.

Before Mark and Dean left, a huge fight broke out between my boys and their cousins over who was right and who was wrong. This fight, started by word of mouth from my dad in prison, turned into a fistfight. It was no longer a word-for-word battle.

A short time after Mark and Dean left, the money in the checkbook went way down. The amount was low enough that Dad told Mom to help the children with money.

Again, I battled anger and rage. I wanted to hate my dad so badly it wasn't funny! All I wanted was for my family to live peacefully without interference, and now two of my boys were separated from the family. And I was too far away to do anything. I was so angry I had trouble concentrating on my job until I had time to cool off.

Dean, my oldest, started taking care of Stephen in the hospital. That left Eddie in charge of the minors at home. Eddie also took over Mark's harness business. Before we went to prison, Mark and Elias always got into arguments about life. Elias tried to make up for the arguments by building a little building where Mark could make harnesses for the community. After Mark got kicked out again, Eddie decided the business was his. Thankfully, Mark found a beautiful family to live with when I couldn't be there for him. I will always cherish that family!

The main reason my dad disliked Mark so much was that Mark was like me. He investigated to see if my dad was telling the truth about whatever Mark was being blamed for or if the story was just Dad talking. Mark started asking questions and discovered that Dad was using Maggie's husband's name and saying that he agreed with everything my dad said. Mark asked Maggie's husband if what Dad said was true, and Maggie's husband didn't know anything about what Dad had said. Dad used the man's name to knock Mark down, and as a result, Mark got kicked out for investigating instead of simply believing whatever he was told.

10

Amelia

AT THE SAME TIME ALL the drama was going on back home, I was finding my way in prison. I had met many spiritually strong ladies who helped me with everything going on at home. And by now, we had a new pastor because the first one had been called to another facility to preach. Our new pastor had prison experience and preached from his own life along with the Bible. He was a great guy, was great with words and wisdom, and spoke truth. He used inmates as examples to get the message across. He'd call inmates up to the front and have them act out the message in person. The result was powerful, and I started attending every Sunday.

Amelia went with me the first couple of times, but all she did was cry and cry. The lady in charge of greeting people walked up to us and asked Amelia what was wrong. Amelia said the message brought back so many memories of how she used to be in church and it hurt her to hear it again. The lady said she would give her a hug except the spirit was telling her not to and she always listened to the spirit speaking to her. The message I got out of their conversation was Amelia was lying about the reason she was crying.

With everything going on in my life, I forgot how jealous Amelia could be. The dress that the laundry department gave me was shorter than Amelia's and went to my knees, which was very short according to our religion. Amelia's dress fit her perfectly, and her English clothes underneath were barely visible. She threatened to turn her dresses in and exchange them for shorter ones. I tried my best to tell her to keep her dresses. I decided if it bothered her that much, I would exchange mine for longer dresses. So I did. I think it made her mad. All I had on my mind was my children and what was going on at home, and I was just happy I had a dress to wear.

After the dress incident, I discovered Amelia had been wearing my white shoes on her days off while I was at work. She'd wear them in the recreation yard and in the lobby and then put them back before I got off work. She thought I wouldn't know because I was working, but unfortunately for her, I saw her walking past the kitchen window when she headed back to our cell. I confronted her about wearing my shoes, and she said her shoes were wet from the rain. Then she threatened to go to the store and buy new white shoes because hers were black, just like Amish shoes. I persuaded her to keep her black shoes because they were a gift from one of the other inmates and were brand new. I told her to not be rude because the other inmate would notice that she bought other shoes. I would've taken the black shoes for myself, but they were too small. Amelia listened to me, but she was upset.

And then there was the lieutenant. Without thinking, I would tell Amelia about what God was teaching me through the lieutenant. She'd instantly know what I was talking about and get mad. Now, nothing ever happened between the lieutenant and me. But God taught me lessons through his actions so I would know which way to go in my life. For example, every chance the lieutenant had, he would walk around me and make a circle. The circle meant God was using a rope to pull me out and away from my evil father. Every circle the lieutenant made, I could feel myself being pulled farther away from the Bergholz community. Sometimes, the lieutenant would walk right up next to me and pass me almost shoulder-to-shoulder. That showed me that God was standing next to me in all the mess and guiding me in a different direction.

I was scared at times because I was being pushed into an unknown place I didn't recognize at all. I didn't understand why God was pulling me away from the community when my children were still there. What would happen if my dad found out I was listening to some stranger and allowing these thoughts to pass through my mind? Plus, this lieutenant was English. What if God's showing me through him to leave my Amish religion and join the English? Yes, I was afraid of all the unknowns, but I thought about the time when I was confused about whom to date—Elias or William. My answer came to me through Jesus standing in my driveway and speaking to my mind as I passed by him. I knew this was the same voice speaking to me through the lieutenant's actions.

Time passed by, and I thought things were back to normal, or as best as they could be between me and Amelia. We went everywhere together—the cafeteria, the recreational area, classes. The other ladies thought it was amazing how we stuck together.

We even made sure we stayed together as cellmates. Now, this may seem strange, and I don't know if it means anything, but in our first cell, I was on upper bunk number two in the very front of the unit. About a month after we arrived in prison, another shipment of inmates came in and the staff moved us to another cell. We went all the way to the back of the cell, and I ended up on upper bunk number two again. That bunk was right beside the closet where the cleaning ladies would get their supplies from, waking me up in the early mornings. I watched for my chance to move, and when two bunks opened in another cell, we moved again. Guess what? I was on upper bunk number two again. What does 222 stand for? I haven't figured it out yet. Amelia and I were always next to each other except for the last cell where we were across the aisle.

A short time after our prison sentences began, Amelia and I started taking classes, a facility requirement to prepare inmates for the real world when released from prison. Some classes were educational, like our GED ones, and others were job-related or for fun, like an art class we took where we made things with tiny beads. I enjoyed the classes. About a month after we started our GED classes, a girl from home called us and said Dad didn't want us to take those classes anymore because we were Amish and didn't need our GED. Dad's attorney had requested that we be exempt from the GED requirement since the Supreme Court had ruled years ago that Amish formal education ended with the eighth grade. After that, we didn't have to take the GED classes.

Moving forward, Amelia and I did a lot of walking and talking. During one of our conversations, she told me she didn't want to go home before me. (She was sentenced to one year, and I had two years.) I couldn't believe my ears when she said that. She even thought about doing something stupid so her sentence would be extended. I knew why she didn't want to go home—the prison ladies treated her way nicer than the ladies at home did. I felt sorry for her because, even with the tension between us and our disagreements, she seemed happier in prison. I also knew that as long as she was there, I might as well not start the countdown for going home because she had to leave before I could start thinking about going home.

11

Dale

WE ARRIVED IN PRISON IN April 2012, and now it was November. Life was looking good for me. I had continued watching the lieutenant and learning from his actions. What God was telling me started changing me, and I could hear and see things from a different perspective. My dad and the church ladies had told me in the past to change my life from the inside out so they could easily see the difference. And that's what I decided to do. What I had been doing wasn't working too well, so I tried doing the opposite just to see what would happen.

I can't explain all the things that I changed in my life, but one example is I started speaking English all the time. And I showered every day. Most Amish do not bathe every day because it takes so much water and creates too many clothes to wash. One of the bigger changes happened when I quit emailing Elias. I told him it was time for me to change my life and I knew I was a child of God. I told him to stop talking to the children because he knew he did us wrong. I explained that I knew what he had done and he knew what he had done. Elias listened and did what I asked. I started telling the children what to do and how to go on with life, and they listened. Things went smoothly until my dad stepped in again and the ladies at home started to butt in. Why? They thought I didn't know what I was doing! I knew exactly what was happening and what I was doing.

Stephen's doctor started calling me instead of Elias, and I made the decisions about Stephen's medical care. He was doing chemotherapy and lost all his hair, which I'm glad I never saw. But the chemotherapy made him sick, and he needed a bone marrow treatment. The doctor called in all of Stephen's siblings to see which one could help Stephen. His brother Dale was the only match for the bone marrow. The doctor scheduled the surgeries for both Dale and Stephen, and then the doctor called me. He explained all the things that could go wrong during and after the surgeries. He said hopefully none of those things would happen, but he had to explain everything as part of their procedures. I was worried but tried to stay calm. How much more could I take? But this was only the beginning of a total nightmare for the Shrock family.

About a week before his scheduled surgery, Dale was making homemade jerky and had to go to the dollar store to get more spices. He was driving the buggy when a drunk driver hit him from behind. At the accident scene, Dale was unconscious and had to be life-flighted to the hospital. Stephen's doctor immediately postponed the surgeries until Dale recovered.

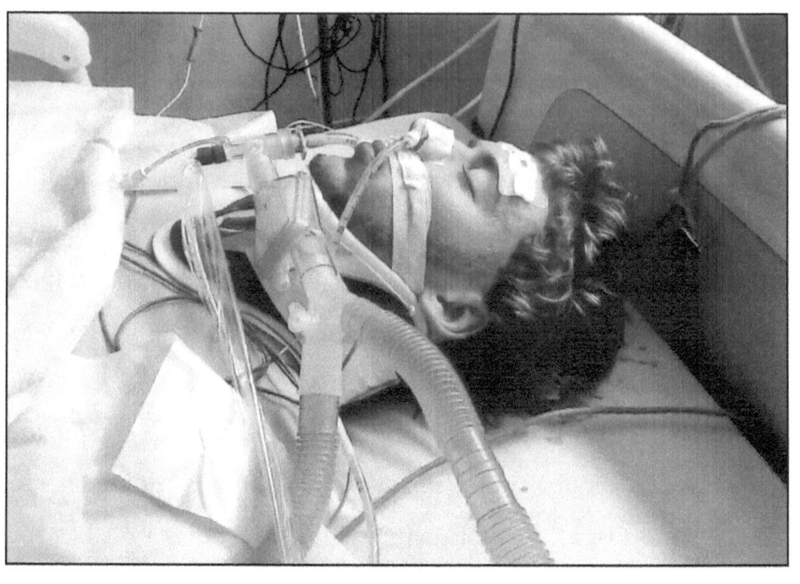

My son Dale in the hospital after his accident.

I will never forget that night. I told the ladies about Dale, and they made a circle around me, took me by the hand, and prayed out loud. I could hear every word they said. I was so impressed because the Amish don't pray out loud, just silently to themselves. While their prayers were being said, I felt a warmth pass through my hands into my body and touch every wound, cut, broken promise, and all the mental abuse. Everything that hurt in my life, except for my heart, was touched, and I felt those areas being healed and put back together again. I knew Jesus himself was inside my body, touching every wound. It felt so good and warm. Something changed in my life, and I knew I could never go back to feeling broken like I did before. I was healed in the name of Jesus. I went to bed that night and slept really hard and peacefully, a first for me in prison.

When Dale regained consciousness, his mind was mixed up. He had no idea he had been in an accident. He thought he was in the hospital for the surgery to help Stephen and couldn't figure out why everything was taking so long. Mark tried explaining to Dale that he'd been hit and his buggy was totaled beyond repair, but Dale didn't understand.

Mark let me talk to Dale on the phone, but Mark warned me ahead of time that I probably couldn't hold a conversation with Dale because his brain was still healing from the accident and it would take time. Dale told me he wanted to go home and hunt again. He was concerned that one of his brothers would take his hunting spot. I tried explaining to him what had happened, but I gave up and talked to Mark again. Dale had to see the smashed buggy for himself before he believed the accident happened and a drunk driver hit him.

The doctor gave Dale about a week to recover before rescheduling the bone marrow surgery. The surgery went well for both Stephen and Dale—thank goodness! Life continued.

We had Thanksgiving dinner in the facility, just like at home. We celebrated Christmas too with lots of good food and gifts. I was surprised, but I was happy.

At the end of the year, I thought about how much had changed already. I'd seen so many things I'd never seen before—lesbians, strippers, jealousy, fights, hatred, besties, friends, loners—all at the same time. It was a lot for the mind to grasp.

12

Preparation

ONE DAY I TOLD AMELIA that since it was getting closer to the time for her to leave and go back home, I wanted to get more confident in myself. I explained I wanted to start doing things alone before she left so I could get used to being alone and not having her around. I thought I explained everything the right way, but I guess I didn't.

Our supervisor came to me one day and said she needed to talk to me in her office. I walked with her to the office, and when she opened the door, Amelia was sitting there crying. I asked what was going on, and the supervisor said Amelia was crying because I was neglecting her and didn't talk to her anymore and had taken some walks without her. I told our supervisor that I had told her I was going to do exactly that so I could gather more confidence before she left for home. I explained how my mind was preoccupied with Stephen's hospital stay, Dale's injuries, and two of my boys leaving the community. I thought Amelia could surely understand all that. We talked, and the supervisor explained to Amelia that I didn't neglect her on purpose. While it was nice having our supervisor's support, it made Amelia mad. And, just like that, the tension between us was back.

Amelia thought I shouldn't be able to handle what was going on in my life at home. She told me repeatedly how her husband went to visit Stephen in the hospital and how Stephen looked very ill. The way she made it sound, Stephen could die any day. I told her I wouldn't believe what she said because my own children and the doctor would tell me if Stephen's condition was that bad.

The tension between us escalated, and she kept saying mean things and trying to scare me with her words. I finally told her I'd had enough and I wouldn't sit with her or walk with her anymore. Things between us got so bad that we had to be separated at work. She worked the morning shift, and I worked the afternoon shift.

The staff had been very kind to Amelia and me and always kept us together in the same cell, but when Amelia verbally attacked me, she was moved out of my cell. That was another blow to me, but I knew I had to go without her soon anyway. The prison ladies saw what was going on and were sad that even Amish ladies fight.

I called my sister Winnie back home and told her about what happened with Amelia, but of course, Winnie didn't believe me. I told her what Jesus was doing in my life, and she made fun of me. Now, I was all alone. I talked to my children still left in the community, but nobody else from home would know what I was going through.

I met another lieutenant around this same time. He crossed my path quite a bit, and I tried to hide from him or walk away from him if I saw him. In my mind, I didn't want to understand two people and figure out what their actions meant. I was worried, but also scared. What was God trying to show me?

(And in case anyone is wondering, the two lieutenants weren't part of my imagination or anything like that. I can give their names to anyone who wishes to know. One of my boys even found their photos online not too long ago, and I instantly recognized them.)

This second lieutenant knew I was avoiding him. He purposely started standing in my way when I had to go places. One night, I was standing behind the cafeteria counter doing my job. I looked up and saw the second lieutenant coming straight toward the counter. Our eyes met, and he shot an arrow straight into the middle of my heart. I felt the arrow go in, and I knew he had me with no chance of escaping. I felt my life instantly change even more. My whole heart felt healed. When the ladies had prayed over me after Dale's accident, the healing went through my whole body except for my heart. Now, my heart was healed. As I sit here writing my story, I can still feel the arrow in my heart.

With my heart healed, I knew I could never turn around and go back to the Amish and live that life again. That door was closed behind me. I knew I had to throw away my old life and embrace my new life coming up.

13

Goodbyes

MY FIRST STEP TO LEAVING the Amish was calling home and telling my daughter to throw away my nametags from my wedding day with Elias. Then I told my son Eddie to gather all of Elias's personal belongings and take them to Millie's house for her to have. I had long suspected Elias was having an affair with Millie, and by all appearances, he wanted her more than me. I felt like God was telling me there would be another guy for me because Elias had chosen another woman.

Everything I had lost was coming back. It started with my thoughts. The breakdown I'd had before entering prison was being healed. I started seeing light instead of darkness, fear, and scary stuff. I started feeling happy again without that fear of being threatened. I actually smiled freely.

One of the ladies gave me a Bible to read and a radio to listen to. When Amelia found out about the radio, she made me feel guilty. Amish aren't supposed to listen to the radio, and even though I had decided I was leaving the Amish, I still felt guilty after listening to Amelia. I gave the radio back to the lady and told her why I was giving it back. She waited until Amelia was at work and gave it to me again. She said she knew I was going through tough times and told me to please take it to listen to and to never let anyone make me feel guilty. So, I took the radio and hid it under my pillows. The music was so soothing. I listened all night, and it felt like healing cream for my whole body!

The time came for Amelia to go home. The ladies wanted me to fix things between us before she left. I tried. I walked to her cell and asked her to talk. She said, "No! Stay away from me." She was the one who ruined our friendship. I realized a person can't fix something in life when that person isn't the one who ruined it. It's impossible.

One night in the cafeteria, the lieutenant stood at the door watching me until I looked at him. At that moment, God said to me, "If you do what I ask you to do in the future, you will get a God-fearing guy for the rest of your life." I knew that statement was a reward and a promise. I also knew, without doubt, it was God speaking to me through the lieutenant. I didn't know what I was supposed to do in the future, but I knew God would show me one day at a time. By now, I trusted him completely.

A short time later, the lieutenant, dressed in a suit with a tie, stood outside my cell. He turned around and looked me straight in the eye and held my gaze until I got the message—God was showing me I would get married again one day. I was happy and excited! Life looked great right now. God had told me what my future held and then he showed me through the lieutenant's actions that the message was legit and real.

Now that Amelia had left, I started my countdown to go home. I couldn't wait to get back to my children. Little did I know that I still had a very tough time ahead of me.

The prisons require certain activities to be completed before a prisoner is released. If you don't complete the activities, you don't get to go home. They need to know that a prisoner can go back out into real life and survive after being locked up. I took some classes to receive the certificates saying I had completed the course to go home.

During one of my classes, I heard some terrible news from the night before. The first lieutenant who had been showing me the way of life fell asleep on his way home from work after a double shift. His truck was found upside down, and paramedics pronounced him dead at the scene from internal bleeding. The story about his wreck was all over the local news. Only people who understand will know the pain and loss I felt when I found out my entire world was smashed again. I felt like my best friend had died. I didn't even know who the lieutenant was. I didn't know if he had a family or anything like that.

Half of me died the day the lieutenant died. Or at least that's how it felt. For days, I forced myself to tell my brain it wasn't true. I couldn't bear the pain. I was terrified that I would fall back into a mental breakdown. I had nobody to talk to about what happened because nobody knew I had grown close to the lieutenant, only talking to each other through silent actions. I didn't tell anyone because, at the time, I thought the women wouldn't understand. Now, I actually believe more women would have known what I meant about how we communicated.

I slowly realized that the news about the lieutenant was true because he never showed up at work again. I cried into my pillow many nights. I had to slow my brain down and stop worrying. I felt so alone and scared with no one left to guide me. I was once again on my own to find my way around. I tried my best to remember what he had shown me. And then God spoke to me again and told me the lieutenant had given me all the chapters of my life. The lieutenant had said all there was to say, and I was to go live my life.

And just when I thought life couldn't get any harder, Dale left the Amish. He took Stephen home from the hospital and asked Eddie to care for him and make sure he was safe. And then Dale left. He called me and told me his plans, and I broke down. How much more could I take? I know we shouldn't ask God why, but I did anyway. I screamed at God, "Why are you doing this to my family? We will never be together again." Why should I listen to God if he kept allowing things to happen that depressed me and hurt me? God answered. He said, "I am not destroying your family. I am fixing them." I did not understand how.

14

Changes

I CONTINUED MAKING CHANGES IN my life. My progress was slow, but I was changing day by day.

I wrote letters home and described to each family what they had done in life. And I wrote to my dad and told him everything that had ever happened that I thought he didn't know about. Little did I know where this path would lead me, but I kept going. Now, I had one more step to take.

The hardest step of all to starting my new life as an Englisher was taking off my headscarf after wearing it all my life. I knew my headscarf was my last tie to the Amish religion. I argued with God for several weeks over it. I told him I couldn't take the headscarf off. I had fought for the covering when I arrived in prison, and what would the ladies say if I just took it off and pretended nothing had happened? That would be insane.

Well, guess what? When God saw I wasn't going to listen to

him and take my covering off, he took care of the problem. We were serving pizza for lunch one day and ran out, so some of the kitchen staff had to bake more. One lady was carrying a pan from the kitchen to the serving line, and when she passed me, the pan bumped my arm and burned it. I heard God say, "Take the covering off. It's time to move on with your life. If you don't, I will do that again." The burn hurt, and I knew I had to listen. The next morning on July 24, my oldest son's birthday, I dropped my headscarf into the trash.

If my sentence had been for one year in prison like the other five ladies, my life never would've changed. I would've gone back to the Amish and my dark life with no escape. My two-year sentence was my door to walk into a new life with a fresh start. I have been reborn again and accepted Jesus as my Lord and Savior. And nobody can take that away from me. He saved me and gave me a pure, fresh start and a new beginning.

The second lieutenant had disappeared soon after he shot the arrow in my heart and before the first lieutenant died in the wreck. I didn't see him for months, and then one morning he was standing in line with the other staff. I couldn't help but think, *Now what?* I couldn't run and hide from him, and I knew I was supposed to watch him and let him lead me. The lieutenant noticed me, and I could tell he knew I changed my life. I was no longer wearing the headscarf or the dress over my prison uniform.

Things made sense now about why the two lieutenants noticed me. God knew the first lieutenant was going to die and I needed a second lieutenant to show me the rest of what God had planned in my new life. The second lieutenant had the same sign language as the first one did, and now I had someone with me again.

I had about six months of prison life left and a new guide. Life was good. I smiled again and felt comfortable. I thanked God for helping me. I also apologized to him for trying to run away from him. He understood and forgave me. He showed me so many things I didn't know before. One thing I will never forget is that you cannot blame anyone for anything unless you have two or more witnesses to testify to what happened. If not, it means nothing.

I was a messenger again for God in my new life, just like in my old life. This time, the feeling was deeper and stronger, and it felt like I was taking a walk into the Bible. I was now a chosen witness for God's Word to testify that he is real and he will change a person's life when and how he wants. There's no running or hiding anywhere. God will find that person, and they will obey him and do as God tells them to do whether or not they want to. They will give up their own flesh and blood and willingly give their life over to him 100 percent.

Maybe not everyone is as stubborn as I was, but I hated pain and was tired of taking hold of good things only to have them taken from me again. So I didn't listen to God right away. But now I gave up everything and told God to take my things and fix them the way he saw fit. I promised to back off because I just messed my life up. I dropped my baggage at the feet of Jesus and allowed him to fix my life how he wanted it done—not my way, but his way.

I didn't know what my future held; all I knew was I was *free* and *happy*. My hair was down and blew in the wind so freely. God had taken all my burdens away.

Looking back at my life, I see a crushed, messed up, broken piece of garbage (me) that God mended together so he could use my life to help others. Amazing how it all happened!

15

Leaving

I LET MY FAMILY KNOW I left the Amish. The first answer I received back from my community was a letter from my dad. He said he was happy for me and all was good. Wow, I was surprised, but what a great reply!

The next week everything crashed. I received another letter from Dad saying that, because I left the Amish, my whole life was a lie, he no longer believed a word I ever said, and he didn't know me anymore. He said those things because he thinks he's God and his house is heaven. He repeated what God will say on judgment day—Flee from me; I never knew you.

My mind immediately went to my children and what would happen to them. I was hundreds of miles from home and knew my leaving the Amish wouldn't come without retaliation. It didn't take long for the ones left in the community to make a move.

I called home and my daughter Eve answered. She said,

"Mom, it happened. The kids can no longer go to school or to Doddy's (my dad) house because you went English!" I tried to comfort her the best I could.

The next call I received was from Eve telling me Eddie packed up all his belongings and left the six minors all by themselves. I freaked out and didn't sleep all night long even though I knew I couldn't do anything to help my children. I prayed very hard and listened to music to calm my thoughts. I was terrified. With Eddie gone, the responsibility for doing chores and cutting firewood for winter fell on Elias Jr., who was only fourteen years old at the time. On our next call, Eve said they slept well and were going on with life the best they could.

In the years leading up to my time in prison, I openly talked about things going on in my life. I ran my mouth about this or that and how what someone did was wrong. I had no idea one of my sisters-in-law was battling a similar fight and depending on what I said. Every time she heard me, Dad would send someone to my house the next day to make me come to his house. He told me I had to explain myself and why I said what I did because it knocked my sister-in-law off her feet and she was troubled. I repeatedly told her I didn't know why I said what I did and I didn't know details about her life, so why blame me?

The fight within the Bergholz Amish Community has always been a spiritual battle. As the days grew darker living under my dad's leadership, my strength became weaker to the point that I had none. I couldn't stand up for myself. My sister-in-law and the other ladies had power over me, and they showed no mercy in how I was treated because of what I had said in the past when people were wrong.

After Elias went to prison but before Amelia and I left for Minnesota, I was kicked out of the community along with all my children. Two of my sisters-in-law went to the school and gathered all my children's belongings and school books from their desks. That night, they knocked on my door, walked in, and slammed all the books on the table. "Teach your own children!" is what they told me. They also said if I couldn't keep up with the school lessons, my children would never be able to return to their school again. What a huge assignment!

I had no idea how I was going to manage teaching my kids. But guess what? Eve, my daughter, was in school at the time and knew all the lessons and assignments. And my son Eddie knew where the teachers got their books, so Eddie and I went to Holmes County to buy teacher's editions to teach the children. We set up desks in our living room, and Eve taught school. After a month's time, we were right on schedule with the lessons, and the children could go back to school. If that wasn't God's help, I don't know what was. And it shut the mouths of the ladies in the community too because they didn't think I could do it.

Sitting here today looking back over my life, I know my husband and my family were serious and determined to shut me up. They involved me in the hair cuttings to lock me away for good. But that only worked in my favor because going to prison was what I needed to finally break away from them and still speak my life story in freedom. Now that I've left their group, I can still talk and they cannot kick me out or punish me because I walked out on my own.

One of the ladies in my cell said to me, "You just swam across the Jordan River, didn't you?" I knew she was talking about my decision to leave the Amish. I agreed with her, and she commented about how exhausted I must feel. And I was. But life looked so different now. I knew instantly that I had left my family behind. I was sad too, but I can't explain the freedom I felt in my heart. God is good, and I started seeing him in so many ways in my life.

My advice to anyone struggling is to just step out of your old life and start a new one without fear because it is so worth it. I know the human flesh doesn't let go so easily and you will face a battle in your mind. I had to face everything I had ever been taught from childhood through my adult years and try to convince myself I had been taught wrong. I knew I could do it, but not without battles in my thoughts.

If you ever want help to leave your old life behind, I will hold your hand and help you across the river to the other side. All you have to do is ask.

Part Three

Freedom

16

Halfway House

MY TIME TO PREPARE TO leave prison had arrived. I knew I would miss the prison ladies who had helped me find Jesus. I hoped we would somehow stay connected once I was outside of the prison walls. The second lieutenant who was guiding me with actions, just like the first one, kept showing me that I was leaving sooner than I thought. I was puzzled by that, but I kept my eyes open. As a mom, I was used to sleeping with one eye and one ear open anyway to protect my children. I was still hundreds of miles away from my children, but I would be home soon to help them.

I packed my belongings, and on September 11, 2014, I left by bus for the halfway house in Weirton, West Virginia. The date reminded me of the tower explosions on 9/11 because I knew I was crashing into my new life. I entered prison as an Amish woman and walked out an Englisher. My new English life officially started that day, and when you were born, raised, and lived as Amish all your life, becoming English, especially after being baptized, was a very bad thing to do in the eyes of other Amish. I knew the next few months would be hard, but I kept telling myself I was walking away from unbelievers. I had thought my family believed in God, Jesus, and the Holy Spirit, but while in prison, I realized they actually didn't.

Going back to soon after I had left for prison, English friends, whom we didn't know we had, came to the community to help out. The Bergholz men had done carpentry work for these people before, so this was their way of showing appreciation. Ron and Dawn Pugh, the couple who had helped my family back when I first left, found out Eddie left the minors on their own with no food, groceries, or money, and they stepped up and helped my children. They took the children grocery shopping and gave them money.

My dad found out about what the Pughs had done and was very angry. He said others were watching from over at his house and weren't going to let my children die. I knew my dad was using my children as a weapon and the abandonment of my children by the community was meant to hurt me. Their goal was to convince me to return to the Amish way of life. However, I knew by now that some in the community didn't want me because they got angry whenever I talked. They also didn't want me to leave, so that meant they were going to try to kill me or hurt me so badly that I would learn to keep my mouth shut. Well, I didn't care anymore. They had made me into a hard-hearted person against evil spirits. I was ready to stand up and fight them to show them they had the evil spirit, not me.

My younger boys in their Amish clothes with Ron Pugh.

When Mark and Dean found out about Eddie abandoning the minors and the Pughs coming to help the best they could, they went back home to take care of the children. I was very upset because Eddie had the nerve to kick out Mark and Dean because he wanted to be the head of the household while Elias and I were locked away. And now when Eddie realized that my children were going to be kicked out, he left them helpless to save himself. I never taught my children to run and leave little ones behind, and Eddie's actions made me angry.

Now that I was out of prison, I could deal with the mess.

Dawn Pugh, Eve, and Elias Jr. picked me up from the bus stop to give me a ride to the halfway house. The ladies in prison had taught me how good it felt to give people hugs, so I hugged Eve

My younger boys just before I came home from prison. They had been abandonded by the Amish community at this point, but still dressed like the Amish.

and Elias Jr. as soon as I saw them. Amish people don't hug each other, and I do not know why. I will never forget my first hug from Eve after not seeing her for almost two years. She hugged me so tight and for so long that I had to gently push her away so we could leave the bus station. I know she was glad to see me, especially after Eddie had abandoned the family and the community kicked them out. We had never spent a day apart until I went to prison, and it felt so good to be together again.

I had told Eve not to send my Amish clothes to the prison because I didn't want them anymore, so all I had were the clothes on my back—a pair of sweatpants, a shirt, and underwear from the prison. We made a stop at the dollar store for clothes, and Dawn and Eve bought me some skirts, T-shirts, socks, and underwear.

My boys shortly after getting haircuts and wearing different clothes.

Although my children had been kicked out of the community, they were still Amish in every way when they picked me up at the bus stop. I sent word from the halfway house to my family that they had two weeks to put my children back in school where they belonged or I would have Mark and Dean cut their hair and give them English clothes to wear.

Two weeks passed and nothing changed. I knew I was headed for a huge fight, but that fight ended up bigger than I expected it to be and got more people involved than I realized it would. At the end of the two weeks, Ron took the children home to his house where the boys got their hair cut and Eve put her hair down. Someone gave them English clothes to wear too.

The next time my kids came to visit me at the halfway house, they looked so different! I barely knew them! It was so good to be able to see more of my children again. Words can't explain it. And my kids were so happy. Eve had a phone that she really liked, and she was listening to music. She looked beautiful wearing pants and a cowboy hat. And she was happy. Of course, she had troubled thoughts over leaving the Amish, but I knew they would leave her eventually.

After the boys started wearing English clothes, my sisters told them that if they put their Amish clothes back on, they would be allowed back in the Amish school again. I guess the community didn't take me seriously before when I told them to take them back to school or I would make them into English people like me. Now that my children were dressing like the English, they knew I was serious. The boys put their Amish clothes back on, and then two of the women came to the house to homeschool the boys. They said the boys weren't allowed in school because of their haircuts. So, my sisters lied to the boys.

I was so proud of my children for taking the huge step of dressing like the English. I knew how hard it was because I had just done it.

Dawn Pugh and three of my boys. She took my boys into her home and cared for them until I came back from the halfway house.

The Pugh family and my children. I am so thankful for how the Pughs stepped up and supported my kids when I wasn't able to.

Dale taking care of and teaching his younger brothers.

17

Eve

LITTLE DID I KNOW MY dad was brewing up a plan. About a month later, when Mark had everything back on schedule again and things were going good at the house, Eddie and my sister Lucille came to the house after dark. They asked to talk to Eve and insisted that she join them outside on the porch. They wanted to talk to her away from Dean, who wasn't going to let her but then decided she would probably be okay. Lo and behold, when she came back inside, she told Dean she was going back to the Amish with Eddie and Lucille. Dean was angry but what could he do? When they called and told me, I was devastated. Because I did as I told my family I would, it cost me my daughter as punishment.

That night when I went to bed, I cried and cried. My heart was broken. My Eve was gone. She was my one and only daughter, and we had been together every day until I ended up going to prison. Now everything was changed.

And then a voice came to me and said, "One day Adam will walk right up to you and, when he does, ask him if you can have his two girls because your sisters took your daughter. Adam will let you have your sister's two daughters." I fell asleep more peacefully after hearing that voice.

The next day one of the staff members told me I didn't have to go to work. She could tell I had been crying and wanted to know what happened. After telling her, I stayed home in my room, rested, and prayed to my God. I didn't know if I would survive this attack.

I found out my dad had written Eve a letter, and instead of sending it to her like usual, he sent Eddie and Lucille over to my house to talk to her in person. He knew Eve would never walk to his house alone, but if two of his people came and walked with her, there was a good chance she would. And she did.

Back when Eddie had abandoned the children, the local sheriff heard about all the confusion going on. He told Mark and Dean to go to court and request temporary custody of the kids. But even with Mark and Dean having custody, my dad continued to give the children a hard time. Dad was still in prison, but he called home and told people what to do.

When Eve went back to my dad's, Mark called the sheriff since Mark and Dean had temporary custody of Eve. The sheriff and Mark went together to Dad's house to find Eve and bring her home. But they couldn't find her right away. I knew my dad was trying to hide her from me. Then they found her at my mom's. Mom had been kicked out of her house and was living in a house trailer on the farm. She didn't agree with how Dad had been running the community, but she was outnumbered since Dad put the sisters ahead of Mom. And then Louisa took my mom's place in her house because Louisa agreed with Dad. Having Louisa and my sisters agree with Dad gave him the power to continue with his evil ways. He used women as weapons against each other to get what he wanted done, but the women didn't see that.

Once the sheriff and Mark found Eve, they talked to her for a long time. They tried to get her to go home, but my mom kept interrupting them to get Eve to stay. You all know by now what would have happened to Mom if Eve had decided to go home with Mark. Mom was supposed to protect Eve from Mark and would have been punished if she lost Eve. Mark and the sheriff finally gave up even though Mark had custody. They said there wasn't really anything they could do to force Eve to go with them. So she stayed.

When she refused to come back, Dean talked to my sisters and told them if they wanted to take Eve they should also take the five minor boys because he and Mark had jobs to do and the boys couldn't provide for themselves. My sisters said they couldn't take care of the boys either. And they said they didn't want the boys, just my daughter, Eve. I always knew they didn't like my children, and this was my witness that what I believed was true. It hurt, but I knew it.

When Eve decided to go with Eddie and Lucille, I was heartbroken. And angry. I knew my dad took Eve on purpose. And I also knew he was using Eve as bait to get me to come back to the

Amish. Eve is my only daughter, and as the only two girls in the family, we were very close to each other. And now she was cut off from me.

While at the halfway house, I worked at a thrift store. The owner of the thrift store had been impressed with the other Bergholz ladies who had been to prison and worked there while they were at the same halfway house. Those ladies had all left before I got there. So, of course, the owner and I talked.

I told the owner all about the ladies who had been there before me and how they all agreed to take my daughter away from me just because I left the Amish. I explained to her why I left too. She told me the other ladies really blindfolded her with their nice stories. They never told her the actual truth about our whole case. They just told her the nice things. She told me she was very proud of me for doing what I was doing—standing up for the truth and only the truth.

Working in a thrift store had its benefits too. The owner knew I didn't have many clothes, so she allowed me to take some home because I did a wonderful job. I was thankful for her kind gesture and for helping me out.

The other people at the halfway house were surprised too when they found out the whole story about the Bergholz Amish. One guy, who was really nice and made sure I felt at home and could find the things I needed, told me the other ladies played card games with him but never told him the story. He said they didn't talk much. Of course, I told him everything. Like the thrift store owner, he told me he was proud of me for standing up for the truth.

Standing up and not lying or covering the truth takes a lot of courage. Not lying was hard, but I can't lie. My fear of lying goes back to that little white puppy I saw a long time ago. When I was seven years old, my siblings and I were taking turns riding a pony around the corn crib. Every time I went on the other side where no one else could see, a mean-faced white puppy came out and scared me! I was frightened so badly. Finally, I said something about the puppy, but no one else had seen him, only me. I was so upset. I quit, went inside the house, and told Mom about the puppy. She said I should listen to Dad and keep my cap strings tied at all times! (The Amish people's rule is to keep your head covering strings always tied. It was considered modern if you left them hanging.) To me, that puppy meant never sin, don't smoke, don't say bad words, never listen to music, never have anything with electricity or a phone, and other things like that.

Fast forward and I can easily see why that puppy experience happened to me at a young age. It gave me a black-and-white perspective on life, morals, and rules. God knew I would stand up for him and him alone. He was using me as a weapon also—just as Dad was using his community people as a weapon. It works the same way for both good and evil.

I knew I would never stop telling the truth. And I could not go back now that I had seen firsthand how evil my family could be.

They were still up to their old tricks.

18

Home

ONE MORNING AT THE HALFWAY house, my supervisor told me that my time had been miscalculated. I was overjoyed! I was going home a whole month earlier than we thought.

Mark and Dean were having a hard time working and caring for the boys by themselves with Eve gone. They had decided to take the boys out to the other Amish communities and find homes for them until I could come home and care for them myself. But, now, they wouldn't need to.

The only problem was my sisters tried to block my house and stay there so I couldn't come home. They sent word to me in the halfway house that I had to look for another home. I knew the halfway house plus the prison facility would not release me until they knew I had a safe place to go to as I would be on probation. I sent word back to my sisters to leave the house. None of their names were on the deed of the sixteen-acre farm where our house was built. The only names on the deed were mine and Elias's. Even though he and I weren't talking at the time and he was still locked up, my house was rightfully mine, and my sisters were not going to stop me from going home. Thankfully, my sisters listened, and they left the house.

In November 2014, Dean drove me home in his little car. When I arrived home, my house was vacant. Again. It had happened so many times over the years.

While I had been gone, Dean and Mark had taken the five younger boys along with their beds and other necessities to their house so they could better take care of them. Mark brought the boys back along with all their stuff, and we were together once more. But it was tough trying to go on with life without Elias, Eve, and Eddie. I couldn't help but remember way back when Elias and I were still together and I had told him one day he would have five of our kids and I would have the other five to go our separate ways. I now had five with me, but the only difference was he didn't have the other five with him. Only two chose to stay Amish. Amazing how that worked!

Because the rest of my family had left the Amish and started a new life with the help of the Pughs, I knew I couldn't turn around and go back to the Amish. Starting a new life was hard. Even my house seemed strange since I had been gone for almost two years.

I was on probation and not allowed to leave my home unless I called the halfway house and let them know. I was permitted to go to the grocery store, but I had to call the halfway house before I left, when I got there, and then again once I returned to my house.

They told me they would randomly call throughout the day or night to check on me and see if I was listening to them. Of course, I didn't want to go back to prison, so I listened. And they told me the probation officer would randomly stop by one day to check on things (I did not know the time and date).

Even with trying to follow all the rules, I messed up. On my first night home, I went to sleep in my bedroom. I was startled the next morning by loud knocking on the bedroom door. I opened the door, and there was the sheriff, Ron, and Mark standing in my kitchen. The halfway house had tried calling all night, and I hadn't answered the phone. Our phone was in the living room, and I had been too far away to hear it. That morning, we moved my bed next to the phone in the living room. Problem solved.

During the first few weeks I was home, we used a battery to run a DVD player so we could watch one movie a night. Dean had to charge the battery again before we could watch another movie. Then Dean gave us a bigger battery that lasted longer. And a couple of months after I came home, Ron and another couple helped us put electricity in the house. With electricity, we had lights and an electric stove and could watch TV whenever and play on our phones with Wi-Fi. Such a change from our Amish lifestyle.

The younger boys started attending English public schools. I had to do paperwork on all five of them. Three attended the local elementary school, and two went to Edison High School. Since I was home alone during the day, I decided to find things to sell for money. Whatever I thought I didn't need anymore, I put on a pile to sell at Rogers Flea Market, one of the largest flea markets in Ohio.

My older boys had been doing so well financially when they were working together as a team at work. And then my dad pitted them against each other and their cousins. By the time I got home, the checkbook wasn't even in one piece and no money was left. I asked Mark to sell some of our horses and the hay off the farm so I could pay bills. Ron and Dawn set me up with food stamps for groceries, and I ended up getting over $900 a month. I was so thankful because I never would have survived without that money. I knew I couldn't get a job until I could drive my own car and who knew how long that would be? I started reading the lessons on how to drive a car. And Dale gave me one of his old phones to practice online courses so I could get my permit.

The burden to support my family fell on me. I knew my dad wouldn't help us financially, and Elias was still in prison and didn't have money either. I will forever blame my dad for the position I was in. He was the reason I sought to leave the Amish in the first place. And he broke us financially when he stirred up the trouble between the boys. His choices and how he dragged the rest of us into them were things I never agreed with. I knew the only option I had was to leave the group because, if I didn't, they would continue to punish me until I agreed with their actions. So the blame is on my dad.

If my sisters would have taken the five boys back when asked, I think I might've tried to stay Amish again even after all the things I'd seen. But when they refused, they opened up all the doors for me to leave, and I was more than ready to go. I was sick and tired of punishments and the abuse of others.

While I was still at the halfway house, I received a letter from Ed, Louisa's husband, asking why I had left our group. He was in prison in Massachusetts, so we wrote back and forth a few times. He expressed how he was still upset with my dad for having a child with Louisa and how he didn't know what he wanted to do when he was released because he didn't feel welcome in the community anymore. He told me that maybe once he was out of prison he would come live with me and help me with my kids. He talked about getting a job and taking my boys with him to work or setting up a sawmill himself so they could work with him. Part of me was relieved that I wouldn't have to travel this journey alone with my five boys.

Two weeks after I came home, Ed called Louisa and told her that he agreed with what I had told him about why I left and the things that had gone on in the community. Later I found out he also said to her, "How would you feel if I got Linda pregnant and you had to see her carry my baby wherever she went? That's what you did to me. You know it hurts me to see you walking around with my uncle's baby in your arms." Louisa got angry at him for talking to me and told him to make a choice—her or me. She also told him he was kicked out of the community for talking to me and was not allowed to call home anymore to talk to her or their children. And she slammed the phone down!

On the same day that Louisa and Ed talked, I received a phone call saying Mom passed away from a heart attack. Ed and I later figured out that she died soon after Louisa kicked Ed out of the community and slammed the phone. To me, the choice Louisa made to kick Ed out and slam the phone was the final blow that killed my mom. Through her actions, Louisa said she chose my dad over her own husband, and that final choice was too much for my mom.

I also blame my dad for Mom's death. He told me he did not get the woman of his dreams, he wasn't satisfied with Mom, and he denied her and purposely put another woman in her place while she was still alive. To this day, I can't imagine the pain and heartache my mom went through. I just can't.

In the evenings when we would gather around the ring in Dad's kitchen, Louisa would attack Mom and tell her in front of everybody that she had no choice but to accept the fact that Dad had replaced her. Louisa would also talk about how it was mom's fault that she got pregnant and how Mom just had to accept the facts. Mom even held the baby just to try to accept it so she could be accepted back into the community instead of always sitting outside and shunned. (She was shunned because she disagreed with Dad's actions.) But no matter what Mom did, she was never accepted back into the group. When she died from her heart attack, the rest of the ladies claimed they had done everything they could think of to help Mom accept the fact that she was replaced, but she didn't accept it, so now it was her own fault she died.

I knew Mom did not like it that I had left the Amish. She hid and protected my daughter from me, and she didn't want to see me, so I didn't even try to go see her after she passed. I knew my sisters wouldn't let me in wearing English clothes because they weren't letting my boys in either. I allowed my mom to rest in peace and wished her well from a distance.

Soon after, Ed told me one of his girls wrote him a letter to invite him back, but in order to go back, he would have to stop writing or calling me. Having him cut off our friendship was very hard on me since he had promised me already that he would stay with me and the five boys. Now I lost him back to the community. I struggled with navigating my new English life alone, but I got over it and moved on.

One thing I learned by watching the situation with Ed was that the Bergholz men were very willing to forget and forgive Ed for talking to me and saying bad things about my dad and Louisa. Their actions reminded me how that's exactly what the other Amish communities tried to get my dad to do so he could come back to their community and start fellowshipping with them again. They told him they would willingly forget and forgive the past if he would apologize for whatever happened before he moved out. But my dad refused to apologize.

19

Trouble

IN APRIL 2015, I GOT my driver's permit. Dale had a truck I borrowed to practice driving around the farm. It was tough learning how to drive, but I stuck with it. Four months later in August, I was licensed and driving my own 2011 Ford Explorer. I had to do the cone test four times before I passed, but I did it.

Now that I had my license, I could get a job. Back when I came home from the halfway house, Dale asked me if I wanted to go to church somewhere. Of course, I did. Dale took me to Grace Point Ministry Church in Wintersville, Ohio (I still attend church there today). I met so many amazing people during those early months. They helped me in many ways with food and fellowship. Some even gave me driving lessons! And one of the church ladies found out I needed a job and got me started with cleaning houses for $11 an hour.

The news spread quickly that I needed a job, and before long,

I had five houses to clean weekly. It felt good to go out, make my own money, and use it the way I wanted to. It took me back to when I was still single and twenty-two. I worked at the strawberry farm making money, but then I got married, and that all changed. I no longer had my own money. All the money I made in quilting went into our joint account and was under Elias's control. Now, I was financially free once more after so many years of being controlled. I still received food stamps for the family, but my monthly amount was lowered because of my job. I had to tell Jobs and Family Services about every change so that they could help me. I was willing to do that and go out there and make a living for myself. I never lied about anything even if it hurt me or took things away from me.

As I gained my independence, people in the Bergholz Amish community started giving me a hard time. Elias and I stored on our property a thrashing machine that he and my brother had bought for the community to use. One day, my brother came over to take the machine to my dad's place. When he tried to move the machine, something was wrong with the wheel, so he took it off. While he was working on it, I went out to talk to him about the machine. I asked for my share of the money out of the machine before he took it away. He started arguing with me, so after he left, I went back outside and put a lock and chain around the wheel and to the shed. I wasn't unlocking it until they gave me money. My brother came back with a check for my share, but he refused to give me the check. So, I refused to unlock the machine. I put the machine in the papers, sold it, and kept the money from the sale.

I was done playing games. I meant business, and my dad wasn't going to treat me the same way this time. The ladies in prison had taught me to stand up for myself and gave me strength and courage beyond measure. (To this day, I am thankful for the ladies I met in prison and what they taught me.)

Time moved on, and more of the men came home from prison. And of course, that meant more trouble for me. Two of the men were plowing the field behind the barn which was property belonging to us. (Elias and I had bought eighty acres from my dad in 1997, but he never gave us the deed to it.) The two men working in the field kept chasing my two ponies out of the fenced area and closing the gate so they couldn't get back in. Every time the ponies ran out to the road, I had to go catch them and put them in the barn. Thankfully, all our other horses had been sold by now or the situation could've been worse. Now it looked like my dad planned to take the property back without giving us our money for it. *Here we go again,* I thought.

Before long, Elias was released from prison. He called the house asking for clothes. I told him he could go ask my brother's wife for clothes since he liked her so much. He started begging, so I said I would put a bag of clothes on the porch for him.

Elias had been kicked out of the Bergholz Amish community for lying about something, so no one in the community would give him a home after he left prison. He walked to a guy's house that he used to work for and sat on the porch steps until the man woke up. The guy asked him why he wasn't at home, and Elias's answer was he shunned me so he couldn't go home.

Elias made it sound like he was too good for home when it was the other way around. If he had straightened up his life and stopped lying all the time, maybe he could've saved his family. His lying was on him and why I didn't want to be with him anymore. Anyway, the neighbor guy allowed Elias to stay in a small building on his property.

One night as I was sitting at the table doing some desk work, the front porch door opened. I looked up and saw Eddie and Eve standing at the door watching me. Eddie said my dad sent them over to tell me, if I came back to the Amish, I could be with them (Eddie and Eve) and Dad would kick Elias out of the community and help me. My reply to them was to tell my dad I would like to have my children back (Eddie and Eve), but I didn't need his help. I could live my own life, and my leaving the Amish took care of Elias in my own way. I knew I was safe from both Elias and my dad. So Eddie and Eve walked away.

Another evening, Eve came walking across the yard with her things. She said she got kicked out of the community again because she couldn't forget her brothers. She had been a mother to them for two years. How could she forget them? She moved in with me again, but my family had turned her against me so much that she called me a b***h. She was angry that I had left the Amish and made life hard for our family. She said if I hadn't done that, the children wouldn't have had to make choices. What she didn't understand was that my dad and Elias were out to kill me one way or another and I had to escape somehow. Then Eve called Elias to come and get her at my house, and she went to live with him in the tiny building at the neighbor's. (Later they found a better house and moved into it.)

Soon after Eve left, I gathered all the leather harnesses to sell, and I realized the pony harnesses were gone. I called the sheriff, and he agreed to help me find them. Except we couldn't figure out where they were. Then I got a note in the mailbox from Eddie saying that Elias and Eve took the pony harnesses during the night. The sheriff drove to their place and made them give them back. On another day, two of my brothers tied their ponies in my barn for no reason. Again, the sheriff came to help and told my brother to take the ponies back and leave me be. Of course, they didn't listen.

Some time went by, and one morning Elias and Eve knocked on my door. Elias asked if he could have his toolbox so he could go to work. I said yes but told him to just take what he asked me for. They also wanted the rest of Eve's belongings. I waited for them to come back from the shed to get Eve's things, but they didn't. I went to look for them, and Elias was piling lots more on the truck than what he had asked for. I confronted him about it, and he said they were his too. I told him that they were, but he didn't ask for all that was on the truck. He could've told me how much he planned to take, but instead, he had said only the toolbox. I made an issue out of this because it showed me that, after being locked up for four to five years in prison, he hadn't changed one bit. He was still a liar and a cheater.

After Elias loaded up Eve's belongings, I asked him to come back inside and make a list of all the things he wanted to keep— we had all the machinery left plus our buggies and more—

because I was going to take our divorce to the court and make it official. Elias looked at me, turned his back toward me, and said, "Kiss my a**."

I thought to myself, "Okay, I will do just that." I put all his machinery and buggies up for sale and sold them within two weeks. Elias found out about it and tried to stop the sales by calling the buyers up and chewing them out. I told the buyers if he called again, to hang up on him. He didn't want to deal with me, so now it is what it is. I would have saved whatever Elias wanted to keep if he hadn't been so stubborn.

Through my actions I was also sending a message to my dad—my choice in life had been made and there was no going back. It's a good thing I changed while I was in prison! I realized I had a tough road ahead because they were willing to fight back to prove that God was with them and not me. After every fight that Dad lost in the court system, he told his community that it just goes to show how strong the devil is, how it's very hard to fight him, and how we can't do it without him. Whenever he said those things, I thought, "So, what Dad is really saying is even God can't control the devil anymore. Yet God was the one who threw the devil out of heaven, and now God can't control him anymore?" Dad's thinking was twisted—he was calling God the devil and the devil God.

A place in the Bible says that when the time is coming, people will get it turned around, and we are there now. I will confess I don't read my Bible as I should, but I still know what it teaches. I can't tell someone to go read a certain verse in the Bible because

I don't know the exact verses and where to find them. I just know it's in there. I'm thinking it all goes back to that little mean puppy I saw when I was seven years old. I stayed with the truth and that's all I know. God started training me when I was very young, and I was a quiet person in my Amish life. I observed and learned all the different ways people react in life. It's crazy and so easy for me to see the difference in choices people make, but when I talk to that person and tell them what I saw them doing, they deny it. Yet I just watched them do it. I kid you not, one of the first things they start doing is throwing stones at me. I can't do anything about it because they talk back faster than I can explain. And all because I reminded them that they are sinners and need to repent.

20

Free

BEFORE I TELL YOU ABOUT my divorce from Elias, I need to backtrack and point out some other things happening while I was learning to stand up for myself.

Besides the daily phone calls and random check-ins from the halfway house, I was required to go back once a week to sign my name and show my face to the staff. My older boys who had left the Amish took turns driving me back and forth each week. God knew what he was doing the day my boys got kicked out of Bergholz. I had cried and cried that day because I needed them to help me at home. I had no idea that my life was going to change the way it did. My plans never included leaving the Amish while in prison, but God knew. And he knew I would need my boys in my new life too.

I didn't mind making the trip back to the halfway house. I enjoyed seeing the people there, and they really liked me. One of the male staff members was hilarious, and he always joked around with us ladies. And he tried to teach us some dancing tricks while I was staying there. I told him I had never done anything like that, and he told me he would teach me, but I left earlier than expected and never got my dancing lessons.

One of my best friends there would take me out to the dollar store to shop for personal belongings. We always got good fresh food at restaurants too. I had my very first Chinese food while at the halfway house, and it was very good. After eating Amish food all my life and then being away from it for so long, eating other foods changed my taste buds. I still miss the different flavors of rice they made in the prison. Amish never have rice as a meal, and instead they eat mostly potatoes and noodles. Now that I am home and have to cook again, my mind just isn't the same on food anymore, but I manage.

After living at the halfway house and going back for my weekly visits, I could easily see a difference between the Amish and English people. Englishers know they do things they aren't supposed to, and they admit it. The Amish cover it up. The halfway house people would tell me about what they'd done and ask for advice to overcome their problems in life. (So very different from the Bergholz community!) Of course, I didn't have all the answers, but I allowed God to speak through me. What helped the most was I let these people know I cared about them and I took the time to sit down and talk. By now I had gone through enough myself to tell others what I did and how I reacted when bad things happened in my life. I let my life experiences and God talk to them.

Many times I thought God had left me in the hands of the devil to destroy me after all things I went through. Those thoughts only lasted so long because God always showed up and showed himself. Every time, I gasped for air when I saw him. I always recognized him instantly. I knew his voice when he called me. A verse in the Bible talks about God's sheep knowing his voice—I am one of his sheep. God allows the devil to do only so much damage and then it's enough and God shows up in a big way.

My troubled thoughts about God handing me to the devil reminded me of the mountains we climb in life. When we reach the top, the view is absolutely beautiful. But then we trip on a stone and down, down we go. Our thoughts push us to the bottom of the valley. The devil loves to attack the thoughts because that's where he can do a huge amount of damage. And it's only human nature to quickly forget how beautiful the top of the mountain is when it's cloudy and the woods we're walking through are so grown up with thorns and bushes that we absolutely cannot see the path. So many times, I've thought about Elisha in the Bible. He was so positive when things went well on top of the mountain, but then it got dark and he lost his way. All he had to do was cry out—"God, help me!" And God came. But sometimes as humans, we forget to ask, so we stay trapped in the valley.

The hardest battle I've fought in my life has been in my mind. Those times my dad took my husband or my children away from me, it hurt. They were my strength, and Dad knew it. He was trying to kill me by destroying my mind so I wouldn't see what he was doing. But with my focus on God, Dad's plan didn't work. My thoughts could not be removed. I see what I see and know what I know.

One day when I went to sign my name at the halfway house, the staff told me it was my last visit. I didn't have to come anymore. Wow, what a relief! I got my probation letter from the federal facilities soon after that saying I had completed my prison life and I was now free. I can't explain to anyone how good, yet scary, that feeling is unless you experience it yourself. I had been carefully watched every day in prison and for my year of probation. Now I had graduated and could experience life freely.

Stephen had come home from the hospital while I was still in prison, but he had regular checkups in Pittsburgh. My boys drove him and me back and forth to his appointments. I met and thanked the amazing doctor and nurses who cared for Stephen and my other kids who had stayed with him. I told them what had happened in our lives and why I left the Amish. I wanted them to understand. The nurses said they wondered what was going on, but nobody would tell them. They didn't want to ask too many questions since the others were Amish people and had their own religion. But now everything made sense to them.

I did not write letters to the ladies in prison as I thought I would. I had to concentrate on my family as they were out to destroy me once more, and I had to focus and keep my mind aware of the situation. My lawyer continued to help me along the way and also the sheriff of Jefferson County. He did an amazing job helping my family.

21

Divorce

THE SHROCK CASE WAS THE last hair-cutting case that happened. And it didn't have to. Elias had been warned by the sheriff and by me not to cut his dad's hair, but he did it anyway. He knew his actions could separate him and me again, and after all the things I went through to get us back together again and start the healing process, he didn't care. He still did it. One can say he did it because he knew my dad wanted him to or whatever may be, but Elias was an adult and he knew better. He knew the risk of being arrested and leaving me alone with all the children. He can say that he figured they wouldn't be in jail for long, but he had no idea it would take us to federal prison. Ultimately, it comes down to the choice he made—and a very bad one at that. Now our family was destroyed with three staying Amish and most of us becoming English.

Elias blames federal law enforcement for the aftermath. He

says it's their fault our family was destroyed. No, it's not. The federal government had every right to arrest us and to stop the hair cuttings. I know firsthand that my dad had plans to do more damage to other people, and someone had to stop him.

One thing that irritates me is I was sentenced to prison and had to pay the price of two years of my life for the hatred of two men and things that happened in their past that they couldn't let go of and that had nothing to do with me. And then Elias wants to blame the federal government. Blame the person who did the crime and the whole story will change. The federal government cannot arrest you if you don't do anything. However you might view my involvement in the David Wengard and Melvin Shrock cases, I deserved to serve my time. The federal government did its job. What I didn't deserve was to be roped into participating just because two men held grudges against others.

Back when Elias cut his dad's hair, he said he did it because he wanted a better life and was hoping it would change everything. In other words, he was trying to please my dad. But like I mentioned in my first book, my dad did not like Elias at all. And Elias knew he didn't. So, Elias was willing to destroy his immediate family to please my dad. I view that as a selfish choice.

I know my dad never liked Elias and never will, but my dad also knows he can use Elias as a pawn against others and Elias will do exactly as he's told because he's afraid of the ax handle. When Elias chose to cut his dad's hair, he became another weapon for my dad.

Why, oh why can't Elias see what happened? It's like he's

blindfolded now and thinks he standing up for Jesus and working for God. But he's not.

After Elias was released from prison, we had to go to court to revoke the temporary custody Mark and Dean held and put the children back in our care. Although I was English now and Elias was still Amish and we weren't living together anymore, the judge released the boys and put the custody papers away.

While we were in session in the court (the five boys were with me), Elias had the nerve to say to the judge that if he gave me full custody of the five boys, he would sue the judge. The judge told Elias that all we did was release the temporary custody from Mark and Dean back to the parents and it was not about fighting for custody between dad and mom. He told Elias that if he wanted to fight for custody, he had to make another case and file for it on another date.

When we were dismissed, Mark, Dean, and I watched Elias walk into the other room to file for custody. I thought to myself, "*Oh boy, here we go again.*" I guess Elias didn't know the community said they didn't want the boys, just my daughter. The next week, I received the custody papers, but before the actual court date, Elias dismissed the custody case. I think he found out what happened before he was released from prison. Again, I know my dad stepped in.

In July 2015, I filed divorce papers in court. I did not make the first move to divorce my husband—he did it that dark night when he held Millie's baby in front of my mom's store. I only put it on paper to make it official. I was finished with that abusive life created by my dad. I was done, done, and done. I realized that my dad and Elias could no longer hurt me. I had God on my side, and I didn't need to be scared anymore. God showed himself in a way that only he could, and I could no longer deny where my help was coming from.

When Elias found out I filed for divorce, he wrote me a letter. He was still living in the tiny building at our English neighbor's place at the time, and he said he was not going to fight for anything. He wrote that he had the tools he needed, he knew why he lost the house and the farm, and he knew it was his own fault. He also said he was going to let me and the children have our house.

And then all hell broke loose. Not long after I received that letter from Elias, he started fighting. I couldn't help but wonder what happened, and then I found out—my dad happened. He allowed Elias back into the community and told him to fight for all he could. I instantly knew the fight was going to be a tough one because now I was fighting the community, not just Elias. It sure seemed like my dad was still trying to destroy me, a goal he's had since I was born. Dad told me to my face that, when I was a baby, he would hold me and I would reach my hand up and pull his beard. He said that made him very angry especially when he got it in his head that one day I would take everything he had. He told me he beat me until I shook all over and was crying with pain. My, oh my, I was only a baby doing things that babies do, yet he did that to me. And to this day he realizes he cannot stop me no matter how hard he tries.

Elias kept taking me into court fighting over the tools. He continued doing this until the judge finally gave him orders to stop nitpicking. The judge called it nonsense and said I could have some things also.

As part of the divorce, Elias said he didn't want visitation rights. He completely denied his own children. He chose my dad over his children because Elias wanted to please my dad and be like him. Little does Elias realize that my dad will never like him, but my dad plans to use him to his advantage. I know my dad and his actions by heart. I grew up beside him, watched his every move, and listened to a lot of things he told me.

And then the news hit that Elias planned to try to take the house from me after all. The judge said since Elias and I both wanted the house, we had to place bids on it and whoever bid the most would get it. Personally, I think the judge made a poor choice telling us to fight for the house without taking our whole situation and history into consideration. There were other ways to resolve who received the house. Knowing I had to bid on my own home, I had the farm appraised. When I got the letter from the appraisal company stating how much the house was worth, I went to the bank to see if they would give me an equity loan to buy Elias's share of the house so I could stay. They said with the job I had they would not be able to help.

My lawyer told me that Elias owed me $40,000 in alimony money, so we could just use that to buy him out. But when Elias turned his income in, it was too low, and the judge said he didn't have to pay the alimony. I found out later that Elias lied about his income. I knew it then too because I knew how much he was making—I was his wife for twenty-seven years, so I knew. If Elias wanted to lie about it so he didn't have to pay, I know one day it will cost him more than money to pay his lying bills. I still believe that unless he changes his life, it will cost him his soul in hell for eternity. It's just money.

Thinking about possibly losing the house, my mind went to the eighty-acre property we bought from my dad but still didn't have a deed for in our names. I decided that, if Elias bought the house away from me, I would use that money to file a lawsuit to get the property. I knew my dad was going to help Elias get the house because neither of us had enough money to go to war over it since we both just got out of prison. Even if my dad wasn't putting any money on the house himself, I knew he was behind it all.

The time came for the bidding to start, and it took place between our lawyers. I had decided to add only $1,000 to every bid Elias made. I figured that would make him the one to up the bid, not me. I knew he was determined to get the house and was willing to pay. In fact, he placed a $20,000 bid every time he bid. My lawyer told me a couple of times I better quit bidding because I couldn't afford to buy it if Elias stopped bidding. My answer was always "No. Keep going." And then we reached the appraisal price. Since I only put $1,000 on top of his bid, I had it. Or so I thought. A couple of weeks passed by and then my lawyer called and said Elias just put in a $50,000 bid. So I kept doing what I was doing.

The final court date came and both parties were in the lobby where we could see each other. I saw the look on Elias's face that said he was going to get the house no matter what. So I watched him and kept putting $1,000 on top until he hesitated to bid. It took him about ten minutes to think about what he wanted to do. I knew there was no way I could buy it, so when he put in the total bid of $230,000 for the house, sixteen acres, and buildings, I let it go. We had a $30,000 mortgage on the house, and the judge said whoever won the bid had to pay off the mortgage. The remainder of the money would be split between us. I was getting $100,000, but I was out of a house and had no idea how to go look for one.

I remembered how, years before, I would walk behind my dad when I was living upstairs above my dad's shop and tell him Elias was going to buy the house away from me and my children and I would be homeless. Dad always said Elias would never do such a thing. Now, I know that was God telling me what was going to happen in the future. And that's exactly what happened, except Dad helped Elias take the house from me.

The public school bus drove down the middle of the community to pick up my children, and Dad and others wanted me out of there so the rest of the community wouldn't want to follow me and do what we were doing. Everyone could see we were happy, so Dad and the others decided to pay the price of whatever it took to get me away from there.

God directed me in so many ways over the years, but since I didn't realize what the future held in those early years, I always got scared and angry at God for putting me in the situations I was in since he was the one who told me to marry Elias. Many times, I was angry, but if I would've understood God's plan, I would not have been angry, but again I didn't know his plan.

— 22 —

New Home

THE JUDGE GAVE ME THIRTY days to find a new home for me and my five boys. I told my lawyer there was no way I could find a house in thirty days, so my lawyer asked the judge for an extension. Thankfully, the judge gave me fifteen more days for a total of forty-five days.

I started looking for homes in the town of Bergholz, which was only three miles down the road from the Amish community. We found one place online matched our living space.

Back when the boys started in public school, I had to get a cell phone so the schools could stay connected if an emergency happened. The teachers were very nice about it, and the local sheriff helped me get my phone. And he bought my boys shoes, coats, mittens, and caps for school. Once I had my phone and was connected to the internet, Dean put me on Facebook. People advised me to not accept friend requests from people I didn't know, but I literally didn't know anyone. I started this new life with only me. I hardly knew my own boys as they had already started their new life and talked differently. But I soon learned.

Because I didn't know anyone, I got scammed while I was trying to save our house from Elias. This guy, who called himself Mark Zuckerberg, said he was sending me a reward for joining Facebook. All I had to do was pay him a certain fee and he would send me $100,000 in cash. And I sent the fee. I regret to this day that I didn't listen to my boys. They had warned me not to send any money to anyone and I didn't listen. I didn't know any better. The money was tempting because I wanted to use it to save our house, and when that didn't work out, I thought I could use it to buy a bigger house. But that didn't work either.

Way back in 1997, Elias and I had bought our sixteen acres of land from Mr. Featheringham, a local real estate agent. When he found out I lost my home, he called me and asked if I needed help finding a place. Yes, I did. So he started looking around for me. Eventually, he found a house for me to rent in town.

When my original thirty days were up, Elias, Eddie, and Eve knocked on my door. Of course, I didn't answer. They taped a paper on my door stating that, if I didn't get out, they would call the sheriff. I still had fifteen days to move, but apparently, they didn't know that. Before long, the sheriff called me and said Elias called him to throw me, the five boys, and all our belongings out onto the street. I told the sheriff that I had forty-five, not thirty, days. The sheriff said that was okay since the judge told me and it was in writing.

Now, stop and think about this—Elias cut his dad's hair and beard for calling the sheriff about Amish business. Yet Elias just did the exact same thing he blamed his dad for doing—involving the sheriff in Amish business—and Elias and his dad were both Amish people. (Sadly, Elias's dad died a couple of months after the hair cutting and is now in his grave with hair like that.) And Elias didn't call the sheriff once, but twice.

Our forty-five days were up, and the boys and I moved all our things into the rental house Mr. Featheringham had found for us. The owners of the house planned to sell the house eventually, and they were really nice people. My house was way smaller now, so I took two huge loads of my belongings to Rogers Flea Market to sell. Even with the house being smaller, we soon made ourselves at home.

When we moved, Mark also moved his little building. It happened to rain the night before, the ground was soft, and the weight of the building left big ruts in the yard. The next day the police came to see me. Elias had called them again and claimed I took too many of the tools with me and I took the bread mixer I had bought from my mom.

Because the police were involved, we ended up having another court hearing over what was or wasn't left at the house. Elias cried big alligator tears to the judge about me taking his tools. I explained to the judge that yes, I did take some tools that were written not to take, but I left behind items of equal value— my Kitchen Queen wood cook stove, a bunch of my canning jars, and my quilt frame. I tried to make it fair. The judge told me to return the bread mixer and a few small things. Then he looked at Elias and told him to stop crying and leave me alone. By now, the judge was tired of us, and I didn't care anymore about what I did or didn't have. Elias fought harder and more severely for his tools than he did for his children.

I walked out of the courtroom that day shaking my head with embarrassment over an Amish man. My eyes had been opened even more to see how disrespectful and rude Amish people can be. And knowing I used to be like that too, I was ashamed.

A couple of days later Mark received papers from the court saying Elias, his own father, had filed a lawsuit against him to take his building away from him. Oh my goodness! And that was after the judge told Elias to stop nitpicking. The court date arrived, and the judge said the amount of money Mark made while Elias was in prison should've paid for the building. And he dismissed the case. What next?

23

The 80 Acres

OUR DIVORCE WAS FINALIZED AND made official in February 2016. As soon as I had my money and was moved out, my lawyer filed a lawsuit against my dad for the deed to the eighty-acre property Elias and I had paid for in 1997 and never received the deed for. And now I was taking another long journey because I knew my dad would fight all the way. He always does.

Not long after my case was filed, I found out Elias had given his share of the property back to my dad in 2015. Elias knew if he fought for his share, he would get kicked out of the community and he didn't want that, so he bowed down to my dad and gave it back. Now it was me and Dad again. And Dad wasn't going to give up the deed.

I told my lawyer my side of the story about how we bought the property and what happened to it. We tried to track down the proof of purchase, but there was none. The banks only kept records for seven years. Since we had purchased the property in 1997, those records were no longer available. My lawyer said there were other ways to get proof. He then traveled to Elkhorn Valley Facility to get my dad's side of the story. He told my lawyer everything, and our stories matched. Next, my lawyer went to Elias and got his story. He told my lawyer everything too and added to it. He said my dad gave him a check in 2015 for $20,000 which was Elias's share of the property. Other than the additional information Elias added, our stories all matched and that's how I got my proof. I still wonder why they both told the truth about it when they could have lied and said we didn't pay for it. They had lied about a lot of other things, and if they had lied about the property, I would've not been able to continue.

Once my lawyer verified our stories, we had a court date to put our proof in writing for the court records. When we were on the witness stand testifying the truth under oath, Elias tried his best to argue with my lawyer, but it didn't work for him. The judge had to tell him to speak up several times because you could barely hear him talk. He said the check he got from my dad for $20,000 came from a church group of some sort. I was mad at Dad for giving Elias half of the exact amount that we had paid for the property twenty-five years ago. The property was now worth way more than that. We had built buildings on it, farmed it, raised crops on it, and fertilized it with lime and lots of manure. But I wasn't going to help Elias fight Dad for money. That was his own fight.

My fight for the property wasn't so much about the actual

eighty acres, but over the oil and gas rights that we hadn't been paid for. Back in 2011, long after we had paid my parents for the eighty acres, they signed a lease with a gas company that paid them about $5,000 per acre. Elias and I signed a lease for our sixteen acres too. But because Elias and I had never received a deed for the eighty acres, the gas company considered that acreage my dad's and he received the money for the eighty acres. Of course, he never paid us our share for that property.

The court decided in my favor and told my dad that he and I were considered joint owners of the property and he was to pay me half of the gas rights money. Since Elias had sold his half of the property back to my dad, the court ruled that he should not receive any of the money. I was told to have the property surveyed and a deed made up, both of which I did. (If you'd like to read specifics about the case, you can find the Ohio 7th District Court of Appeals opinion at this website: casetext.com/case/shrock-v-mullet. Note that the web address was correct at the time of publication.)

Once the judge made his decision, my lawyer told me that my boys could go on the eighty acres whenever they wanted without a problem. And they did. Nobody said anything about it. The boys even hosted a few gatherings on the property without incident. And then another time the boys went down there, and things didn't go so well. Some of the Amish waited until after midnight to see if the boys were still there. As four people at the gathering went to get in their vehicles, the Amish were there waiting with chains. They beat the four up so badly that the girl had to go to

The picture may not show the details well, but his sweatshirt is ripped from being beaten by the Amish with chains and his body is covered in bruises.

the hospital and stay overnight to be checked out. The others had bruises all over their faces and bodies. The next day I took two of them to the sheriff's office to report the beatings. Except the sheriff's office did nothing. The sheriff said the deed wasn't signed yet and that allowed the Amish to get away with it.

I was learning how corrupt the system was. All the sheriff had to do was lock them back up again, and they would have left us alone whenever we were on the property. We never went down there to harass them. But it was easier for the sheriff to tell us to stay away until the deed was signed even though the judge had already made his decision and we had permission to be there. In fact, the Amish had called the police to come out and chase the boys off before they used the chains, but the police refused to come out. My brother called another county sheriff, but they didn't do anything either because my boys told them the judge said it was okay. When that happened, the Amish took it into their own hands to beat the four with chains.

My dad fought the county court's decision all the way up to the state supreme court. And even then, he refused to give me my court-ordered $200,000 for the gas rights. When he refused, my lawyer filed paperwork to put all eighteen hundred acres of Dad's property up for sale. We planned to call out auction sales and sell off the property until I had my money. My brother had to go to the court to pay off the ad to sell the property. And within two days, I had my check. After paying a lot of the court costs and paying my lawyer, I received less than 30 percent of the original $200,000. But that was still a nice chunk of money.

In June 2021, my lawyer filed papers to give the judge the right to sign the deed in my name as my dad was too stubborn to sign off. Now I have an official deed for the eighty acres showing I am a joint owner along with my dad.

I found out that the Amish had put trail cameras out around the property to catch the boys doing things, but the cameras won't do any good now. I own just as much right to that property as my dad does. My life started to quiet down after the deed was signed because the police were no longer called and obligated to report to me what the boys were doing. Life became peaceful.

24

Stories

MY NEW LIFE OUTSIDE OF the Amish community was exciting. I met so many new friends and people. Everyone seemed to like me, which surprised me. I had been told for years that I was a bad person and would go to hell for my behavior. I knew that was a lie, but it was still odd to have people liking me and helping me.

I was now the one driving Stephen to Pittsburgh for his checkups. I couldn't believe that an ex-Amish woman was driving through Pittsburgh when even some English woman wouldn't drive through all that traffic. It reminded me what all moms do for a child they love—extraordinary things!

A couple of months passed, and I didn't want to pay rent anymore. Mr. Featheringham found me a house for sale in town for $51,000. He helped me out with $11,000, and I had enough to pay the rest of the house off.

I was still cleaning houses for eleven dollars an hour and working about five hours each day. One of the houses I cleaned belonged to a friend of ours who was involved with the Bergholz Amish families in many ways. She told me a lot of things I did not know. One story she told me was about my sister Emily who had pancreatic liver cancer. When Emily was sick, she was searching for help and answers. She didn't want to just take my dad's word for everything as she was facing death and was scared. So Emily would take her Bible to this lady's house so the lady could teach her about the Bible. Emily said she didn't know who Jesus actually was and she really wanted to know, especially since she was dying. Emily was sneaking behind my dad's back while doing this.

Emily also asked the man of the same house to take a picture of her and save it so he could give it to her children when they grew up. She wanted her children who were quite young at the time to remember her. The man said he couldn't do that as he still respected the Amish the best he could. Later, after Emily died, he found out my dad had asked his two lawyers to interview him and Winnie and post it on YouTube. He wanted to tell the world that Adam and the sheriff took Winnie's two daughters from her. They even used a photo of my brother in the video. When the man found out about the video, he cried his heart out because it would've been okay for him to take that photo of Emily and keep it for her children. But now it was too late.

The lady told me a story about my mom that shocked me in a way. Mom had a bulk food store. Amish people bake all their food and cook huge meals. We had big gardens and stored up potatoes for the winter—the same as storing hay for horses to eat in the wintertime. Elias and I used deer meat for all our meat, and other families used beef. We also butchered our chickens for meat at the end of the year and got a fresh batch of chicks in the spring to replace old laying hens. We canned our fruits and vegetables every year and made soups of all kinds.

With all the cooking and baking we did, we had figured out that regular store-bought flour did not make good homemade bread dough. The bulk flour that Mom carried in her store did much better. But sometimes our bread dough didn't rise as it should have. We ladies tried to figure out why because the bulk food flour always made good bread without fail. Mom sat in the middle of our group helping us figure out why the flour didn't work right.

This lady told me that my mom would sometimes mix store-bought flour with the bulk food flour to save money. Instantly I knew why the bread sometimes did not work. Mom sold us the mixed flour at the same price as the regular bulk flour. She was a crook. And she knew the whole time why our bread wouldn't work the best. She also knew she wasn't allowed to mix the flour too often or we would have suspected.

If that story didn't shock me, one of the stories the lady told me about my dad knocked me off my feet. I wondered why I had to leave the Amish to find out what my family was actually doing. She said my dad visited her family and tried to get her to bow down to him so he could control her. This lady told him she would never bow down to anyone but her Jesus, her Lord and

Savior. Dad also told her that one of the ladies in our church was a whore. This lady's married daughter walked right up to him and said there was only one way he could possibly know that she was a whore and that was if he had slept with her. Dad got so angry his face turned red and he started to foam out of his mouth. He was trying to get these ladies to believe his lies to manipulate their minds and it wasn't working. He went outside to where the horse he drove was tied to an oil tank. He was so angry that he ripped the rope off the tank hard and fast enough that he broke the spigot off the tank. The family lost fifty gallons of oil that day. Later Dad stopped in and paid the family for the oil. He never told anyone in the community what had happened.

I had been cleaning houses for some time when a few of the ladies got smart. They called me to help them deep clean one or two times, and then they said they didn't need me to come every week. It made me sad. And it was getting harder to find houses to clean.

The oldest of the five boys who lived with me was starting to drive. He got a job and bought his first SUV-type vehicle. It didn't have a muffler on it and was loud. Twice the neighbors called the police to warn us about the vehicle. Because we were living in town around so many people, they asked us to get it fixed, which we did eventually. We were country folks trying to adjust to city life. It was tough to get used to, but together we survived.

25

Adam & Eve

AFTER WORK MOST DAYS, I took a walk up the road and back for something to do. One late afternoon about two years after I had been home, an Amish man and a girl were walking toward me. I had no idea who they were. I hadn't seen most of the Amish for four years—two years while I was in prison and two years since I had been out. I didn't recognize these two people until the man introduced himself. Turns out it was Adam and his sister. I got goosebumps when he told me who he was.

I instantly remembered the voice I had heard in the halfway house when the Amish took Eve away from me. The voice said I needed to ask Adam if I could spend time with his girls since my girl was taken away. And if I asked, he would allow me to have them and he would agree that I could probably be a better mom to them than my sister Winnie.

So Adam and I started talking after we met along the road.

We put a lot of the puzzle pieces together as to what happened when I was still Amish and going through the different court trials. We went as far back as 2005 when we drove Adam to his parents' house and dropped him off. I told him all about our side of things and what was said and done. And he told me his side.

Adam said one of the main reasons he got custody of the girls was because Winnie told him what Dad's next move would be so Adam would know exactly what to do on his part. And since the sheriff had dealings with my dad, he already knew how manipulative he was. Dad tried manipulating the sheriff's mind so he wouldn't remember exactly how things happened. It didn't work, plus the sheriff helped Adam get the girls by putting a good word in for him to the judge.

Adam also explained his side of the story about why he went to jail and what happened. He told me about how he had bought timber on some property to cut and sell. He didn't realize the guy living in the house was a renter, and Adam gave that guy the check for the timber instead of paying the real landowner. The renter took the check and left. When the landowner found out that Adam paid the renter for the timber, he called the police and had Adam arrested until they figured out exactly what happened.

Dad told us that he bailed Adam out and that he should've left him in jail to prevent him from taking the girls away from Winnie. Except Adam said my dad never bailed him out. And now Adam was telling me that he was never in actual jail with the orange clothes on. He was just in the office being questioned by the law, and the sheriff planned to let him go. Adam's story was way different from the story Dad had told us.

Another story Adam shed light on happened when Winnie went into the courtroom to ask Adam to give her the girls back. She sat on his lap, kissed him on the neck, and never asked him to give the girls back to her. The courtroom had cameras in it and the sheriff watched everything from his office. He saw for himself that Winnie still loved Adam and everything was all my dad's idea to separate them, not Winnie's idea. When Winnie walked out of the courtroom that day, she was crying and shaking. She told us that Adam refused to listen to her and give her daughters back to her. Except now I know that was all a cover-up because she actually told Adam that it would be better if he had the girls because she didn't want them to be close with our dad.

Why would I believe what Adam was telling me years later? The main reason is Winnie and I used to sit behind Dad's house in the evenings and she'd tell me her true feelings about how she felt toward Adam. She still loved him, but she knew she wasn't allowed to let Dad know she was still in love with him. All she could think of was she just wanted to be held and kissed by him. She asked me if that was bad or good. I told her if she truly believes that he's a demon, like she's pretending to say, it's bad because we shouldn't want to be held by a demon. But if she doesn't believe he's what she was saying he was, it's a good thing and how she should feel. Adam said Winnie always told him that one day they would be together again and he would always be her husband no matter what Dad said.

The whole picture changed in my mind. Puzzle pieces were being put together. I wrote my dad a note and told him what Adam told me. I never heard back from him, and I assume he covered up for Winnie and called Adam a liar. Adam wanted to go back and tell the community his side of the story even when he knew nobody would believe it. He never got that chance though. Dad made up the story about Adam and his mother, and Adam was stuck with that story typed on his back forever in the Bergholz Amish community.

In March 2020, my dad arrived home. Because of the coronavirus pandemic and my dad's age and health conditions, he was eligible to participate in a special program allowing prisoners to serve the rest of their sentences at home on home confinement. When we had appealed our case and the judge dropped the federal hate crime charges, Dad's sentence was reduced from fifteen years to ten years and nine months. He was credited for time served before our trial, which made him eligible for release in January 2021. Prior to the pandemic, Dad had already been moved to a halfway house, so they just moved him home.

About eight weeks after Dad arrived home, the whole valley exploded.

My cousin Ed, Louisa's husband, was kicked out of the community. We all knew that was going to happen anyway as soon as Dad got home. Dad gave Ed three choices—go to their ninety-one acres and live in a tent, live with the pigs, or call me and leave the Amish. Dad hated that Ed would talk back if he disagreed with Dad's orders. And the solution, in my dad's eyes, was to banish Ed to somewhere else. Ed called me. I picked him up from the bridge and brought him to my house. He looked like a ghost.

Dad had been giving him a hard time to the point that Ed hadn't eaten or showered in days and he couldn't sleep. He had one clean set of clothes and his pocketbook with some cash in it. While he took a shower, I cooked him some eggs and bacon with toast and coffee. Afterward, Ed went to the gas station and got some sodas to drink. Within two days, he was feeling better and starting to get his strength back.

We talked quite a bit, and I found out that he was blaming himself for everything that had happened. I talked to him, pointed out things that happened, and gave him my side of the story. I also made it clear to him that nothing was his fault. It was my dad's fault. My dad wanted Ed's wife, and I knew even if Ed would've lived a perfect life, my dad was going to prove a fault on him even if it was a lie to kick Ed out and take his wife.

The final straw involved Ed and his sawmill business. He was cutting trees for my dad and had made a deal with him on money. Well, Dad blamed Ed for not paying him the right amount of money. Louisa kept track of Ed's paperwork, and Louisa and Ed went back over all the figures trying to find the mistakes. Dad kept saying, "I sure hope I am wrong and you don't owe me anything." As I listened to Ed's side of the story, I already knew what my dad's next move would be. They couldn't find any mistakes, so Dad said, "It took you too long to go over it all. Get out of my house now. You are not going to sit here and tear my church apart." Louisa heard it all and knew my dad was lying. But she didn't stand up for Ed. Instead, she watched him walk out the door. Ed told me he wasn't going to waste any more of his time fighting for her because she didn't want him.

What my dad didn't know was Ed had met friends in prison. These men had gone on the computer, found our case, and found out what my dad did to Ed and his wife. They asked Ed if what they read was true. Ed tried to cover up for my dad, but the men were not fooled. They saw in his face that what they said was true. All of them gave Ed their phone number in case something happened again after he got home and he needed to call for help.

When Ed got home from prison, he went through his things and threw away all the phone numbers except one. Ed called that guy and asked if it was okay if he came to his place because he got kicked out of my dad's community. The man had a lobster business in Maine, and he paid for Ed's plane ticket, prepared to meet him at the airport, and gave him a home and a job.

Stephen and I drove Ed to Pittsburgh to catch his flight to Maine. And off he went to start putting lobster traps in the water. We bought him a cheap phone from a dollar store so he could keep in touch with us and with his new boss. Before he got on the plane, Ed told me he was going as far away from my dad as he could—all the way to the ocean. That's as far as he can go.

26

Work

I QUIT MY CLEANING JOB and started working at a local fast-food restaurant. My new job was better than cleaning except for days when we were short of help or someone didn't show up. On those days, I covered for two people but worked for the same amount of money as one person. Slowly but surely my strength started to go downhill from being overworked.

I tried complaining to management but got no extra help in the prep line. During my first year, either I did the work of two people or my hours got cut. In a way, I felt like I was being abused. I needed the money from the hours I was assigned, but they didn't care. Several times I asked for a raise or to move to another area with better pay, but nobody paid attention to me. The other workers were offered management positions, and the restaurant continually held classes in the lobby for people to learn more and receive better pay. Not once did I get the offer to take a class or get the paperwork to fill out to move up in my career. I finally realized that they were ignoring me on purpose because nobody likes to work in the prep area. If I moved up in my career, they would have nobody to do the things I did. I fought against the negative thoughts daily. By the time my shift was over, I was exhausted from thinking, running errands, and doing my job.

I wanted so badly to leave the restaurant, except I didn't have my high school diploma or GED, so my job opportunities were limited. And then I found out that the restaurant company offered online classes to get a high school diploma. I bought myself a laptop and started the classes. An academic coach called me once every so often and emailed me with "Good Job" stickers to encourage me to keep moving forward.

It was tough to keep up with the classes and work and keep my household going with cleanliness, food preparation, and grocery shopping. Somehow, I managed. Because the restaurant started shorting my hours, I also signed up for another job to work in the deli at a Bergholz gas station. I would come home from the restaurant, rest for an hour, and then do seven to eight hours at the gas station. And we were short of help there too. Lots of times only one person did the preparation for the next day, filled out orders, took phone call orders, cleaned, put all food away for the next day, plus washed all the dishes.

I worked both jobs for a year. It felt good to work for the money, but it was also exhausting. I don't know how I survived, but I did. My feet started to hurt after standing on concrete floors all day long.

Since I was working two jobs and making more money than when I was cleaning, our food stamp money was decreased. At the end of that year, I quit the gas station job and got my food money back on the card. What did I gain working two jobs for fifteen to sixteen hours a day when the amount of money I was making at the gas station was the exact amount of food money we lost?

Once I went back to one job, I had more peace again. I finished writing my first book and continued working on my high school diploma. I could not do the math, so my boys helped me out with that. (I had permission to let them help me!)

While working at the gas station, something special happened. An older lady came in frequently to order a special salad she wanted me to make for her. She said I was the only one that made it like she wanted it and it was always delicious. On my days off, she wouldn't order the salad until I was back again. That made me feel special.

One nice night, my brother-in-law's oldest son and his wife stopped in. I had no idea who he was. Children change so much when you don't see them for a couple of years. He said they just got married and were on their honeymoon. He brought his new wife to the area to show her where he used to live. That was funny.

In the middle of everything else going on, the boys had another party at the eighty-acre property. My dad was out of prison now, and I know he was behind what happened next because almost everything had been quiet while he was locked up. While the boys were on the property, an open buggy with four or five people came along. One of the people was my oldest sister, Maggie. My brother started openly accusing my nephew of sleeping with his mom, my sister Maggie. My brother said my dad saw animals doing dumb things together. When one of the animals looked at Dad and smiled, Dad knew my nephew was sleeping with his mom. Yes, I know it doesn't even make sense at all. Dad was the one who saw it, and it was probably meant for him since he was the one sleeping with other ladies from the church. Anyway, the other people on the buggy kicked Maggie off and made her stay there while they went home.

Maggie didn't want to go with the boys, so she walked home from the eighty-acre property. One of her boys who had left the Amish drove behind her in the truck to make sure she got home safely. But that wasn't the answer to her problem. Next thing we knew, the community kicked her out and refused to let her back in. She called me and told me to ask her boys to come get her and take her to the English world, our world. So they did. She put English clothes on and cut and dyed her hair. She shaved her legs and her face. (She was very hairy since the Bergholz Amish were not allowed to shave. They believed that if God gave you hair, you must leave it like that. But the men and boys were allowed to get real haircuts.) About three months later, Maggie had a job and was ready to start her driver's test to drive a car when her husband called her and asked her if she wanted to come back to the Amish. Within five minutes, she left all her English things behind and was on her way back to the Amish.

I couldn't understand why she would want to go back. They

never liked her and treated her like crap. But going back was her choice. And as of today as I am typing this, I haven't heard a word from her since she went back.

No one in the Bergholz Amish community is allowed to communicate with anyone else outside the community. Why? They would find out my dad is lying to them and he doesn't want them to know. What a shame. That community has nothing to do with God or the devil—it is controlled by my dad. Dad is using God and the devil's name to manipulate the people still living there so they don't move out and away.

In February 2021, I left my job at the restaurant. My dad and some of the ladies had started coming in and making scenes whenever I was working. I told my boss about it and she chased them off, but Dad just continued by sending others in. Knowing he wouldn't leave me alone, I went on the Indeed website and started looking for jobs. I found one in a warehouse in Pennsylvania where I work behind locked doors and no one is allowed in unless they have a key. I work the late shift, and I have to fight off sleep on the hour drive home because I don't get off work until after midnight. But I feel safe once more, and I am home during the daytime to do my cleaning, laundry, and other chores.

27

Videos

ONE DAY I WAS SITTING in my kitchen talking with my son Stephen and his girlfriend when a lady walked behind my house and across the yard. She knocked on my back door and asked if I was Linda Shrock. I told her I was and asked her why she was asking. She told me her name was Miki, that she lived near some Amish, and that they were doing weird things. She also said she was looking for Ed who had left the Bergholz community. She said two men in white clothing had walked up behind her house and told her where to find me and that I would tell her how to contact Ed.

I told her that my dad was the bishop in the community near her and that, yes, he does things. I briefly told her some things that had happened, and I handed her my first book to read so she would trust me and know that I was telling her the truth. She instantly knew I wasn't lying to her and said her knees were shaking so badly that she had to sit down.

As we talked, Miki explained how she had known other Amish before, but they were nothing like the ones in the Bergholz community. Then she told me a story about hearing a child screaming one day and how she went outside to investigate. She watched my dad chase a little girl up a driveway. Miki drove over to see what was going on and found the little girl crying.

Later, she saw my dad, Louisa, two girls, and a baby in a buggy at the gas station. She approached the one girl and asked her why she had been crying like that. The girl said it was because she missed her dad. Then Miki asked her who had cut her hair. (Miki told me that the girl's hair was chopped up, not a nice haircut, and looked awful.) The girl pointed at my dad and said he cut her hair. My dad's response was "Nobody will cry around here unless it's about me." And then he walked away. According to Miki, this girl's choppy haircut wasn't the only one she'd seen like that either.

After talking some more, I told Miki that we could try and do something about what was going on, but it would be tough because the sheriff didn't want anything to do with the Bergholz community. I thought his recent actions very strange because I had known him throughout the entire fight and he would do anything to help, especially any of the kids and me. He'd always made sure we were safe, but now all of a sudden, his words changed, and he sounded different. I was confused. (Later, I would find out why he changed.)

Miki and I decided to contact the sheriff's office but discovered the sheriff had transferred the Bergholz Amish case to a lieutenant. The new person in charge told Miki that before the department could act on anything, the event had to be recorded. Of course, Miki didn't record what she saw or her conversation with the girl. I was puzzled because needing recordings and all that just didn't sound like the sheriff and the department I knew.

What I didn't know at the time was this new dilemma pointed back to Adam. As I mentioned before, Adam and I had talked about a lot of things as friends, or so I thought. I hid nothing on my side of the story, and I trusted Adam a little too much. Over time, I realized he made a liar out of me. He had told me to tell my sister Winnie that I could be a mother to her girls since she didn't want them anymore. So I drove to my dad's driveway and asked to talk to Winnie. She about went haywire screaming at me to leave. I told her what I wanted and said I would leave once I was ready to leave. She said my having her girls didn't matter because if she couldn't have full custody, she didn't want them. After that, Adam never let me have the girls. I was allowed to visit them at their home, but they never stayed with me in my home. I knew I had lied to Winnie because of what Adam promised me and I don't lie to anyone.

Adam also told me he was going to put all the gifts Winnie had ever sent to the girls on a pallet and send them back to her. He would keep the letters she wrote, but the gifts were being sent back. I asked him if I could write Winnie and tell her that Adam was sending her a present that she would enjoy for being such a great person and kicking people out of their homes and onto the streets. Adam agreed, but again, he didn't do what he said he would, meaning I lied to my sister. At that point, I decided I'd had enough and wasn't going to tell my family anything more about Adam since he never kept his word. He had told me enough through his actions that I knew he had a lot of dark secrets in his life that had never been exposed.

Miki came back to visit me, and we continued talking about lots of things from my past. I told her I'd heard about an ex-Amish person who does live videos to help people who'd left the Amish, the Mennonites, and other cultures. His goal is to help them overcome the abuse in their past and get started with their new lives in their new world. Once a person walks out of the only life they've ever known and what they've been taught as a child, it's hard mentally because now they have to turn their boat around and paddle against the current of their own beliefs to get a fresh start in life. This person I remembered who does the live videos helps people who want help. Miki recalled the name of the person I was talking about—Eli Yoder. She messaged him on Facebook and he was instantly interested in exposing the Bergholz community even more than it already was.

Miki and I did an interview with Eli and posted it on Facebook. I know my dad won't accept help from anyone, but we thought our interview would make him move in a direction that could help save the Bergholz children from the exact same abuse of hair cuttings and beatings that the adults took before our federal court case and prison terms happened.

Miki and I called Ed and told him about the video. He called a friend of his and asked him to give his number to one of the Amish to call him. His hope was that he could get the Amish person to talk about what was going on in the community. The Amish person refused to take the number, but then later this person called Miki and said he changed his mind and wanted the number after all. Miki refused to give the man the number because she knew he had talked to my dad and figured out that Dad was the one who wanted the number, not the Amish person.

Our video did cause people to react, but the results we got were unexpected. An FBI agent came to my house to talk about what had happened. Again, I was told that since we didn't get the events on video, the FBI couldn't take any action. To me, that was unbelievable. My dad is on record with his actions and what he does when people under his authority refuse to listen or they do something he doesn't like.

Then Adam called Eli, Miki, and me. He accused me of purposely doing the video to make the sheriff look bad. His accusation wasn't true at all. I clearly said in the video that I was at the sheriff's office several different times asking him to do something about my dad, to keep him in prison for his full sentencing, and to not allow him to go back to abusing people again. The sheriff told me that day there was nothing they could do and they had done their duty. I understood what the sheriff explained to me, and I left knowing and trusting that the sheriff told me the truth. The sheriff had helped me out a lot when I needed him and I respected him for that and for always telling me the truth.

When Adam talked to me about the sheriff, he made it sound like the sheriff was upset with me. Curious, I asked Adam if he had watched the video himself or if he was just going by what people had told him. Adam was Amish so he wasn't supposed to have internet service, and it would be impossible to watch the video without internet access. Adam admitted that he hadn't watched it. So I told him that as long as he didn't watch the whole video, he couldn't call me up and give me orders on what I should say and what I couldn't say.

Another part of Adam's story that bothered me was when he told me how he went online and researched the person who made the video for us. He said he found the man and knew his family. Adam's advice to me was to stay away from the man and not talk to him. That made me instantly angry. First, there was no way on earth I was accepting advice from an Amish man who was breaking the rules and not supposed to be on the internet at all. Second, in my opinion, no one, including Adam or any other person, has the right to research someone's history and judge that person because of his or her background without talking directly to that person.

I asked Adam a few questions and discovered that the person he found was not the same person we talked to. However, Eli, the man who videod our interview, did have a hard life. He used to be a drunk and a rough person, but he found Jesus, changed his life, and is working for God exposing the hidden evil in people's lives. He helps people break free of the devil's chains.

Adam then called Eli and ordered him to stop making the videos. Adam claimed Eli lacked permission and the rights to create the videos. What Adam didn't realize is Eli has permission if the other person is willingly cooperating with him during the interviews. Adam has no capacity to order someone to stop their actions. Eli's response to Adam's demand was to tell him that a prayer meeting was scheduled at Miki's house. (Eli is all about praying for people and their freedom.) Adam told Eli to stay away or he would personally call the sheriff and have both parties arrested and questioned. Adam also said prayer was stupid. His statement surprised me because I thought Amish are all about prayer, or so they say.

Then Adam called Miki claiming to be an FBI agent and a lawyer. He told her he had the right to give her orders and tell her what to do. He told her to stay away from my dad and only talk to him (Adam). He also said to not talk to Eli or Linda, only to him. Then he started warning her of the evil the Bergholz Amish do down in the valley. All the things he told her were the things I had told him thinking I was talking to a friend. I had no idea he was going to use that information for his own personal gain.

How do I know that Adam's story to Miki was what I had shared with him? Adam never saw or experienced any of the abuse the Bergholz Amish went through. He was not there. He left the community back in 2005. The family separations, the chicken coop episodes, and eventually the hair and beard cuttings were a result of the custody battle over Adam and Winnie's girls. He was already gone for those things. So the details he shared came from what I had told him. Now he turned around and used that information against me. He told Miki that my story was a lie and to not believe me because I was one of the Mullet daughters. Stabbed me right in back. Had I known he was going to do this, I would've never told him anything.

The lieutenant from Jefferson County who now oversaw the Bergholz Amish case also called Eli, Miki, and me. What he told us to do was completely different then what Adam was saying. Adam had told us that he was working with the sheriff's department and had a right to give out orders. Adam claimed the sheriff's team had seven people on it and, whenever a call came in, they would talk about the call and have him tell them what he would do. So, basically, what Adam was saying was that the sheriff didn't run the show anymore, Adam did. Nothing made any sense at all, but I could see what had happened, and I was angry.

Before I met Adam on that night he walked toward me, the sheriff and I had been working together one-on-one with my family and he was helping me in so many ways. All of a sudden we couldn't understand each other, he didn't want to help me, and I knew something was wrong. Now I had my answer—Adam. He stepped inbetween me and the sheriff and made the rules about what he wanted done with my family and not what the law wanted to do according to what Adam was saying.

I set up a meeting with Adam and called him out on all the things he did out of order. I also know the law and how it works. First, if he were truly a lawyer or an FBI agent, he needed to show proof. He refused to show his badge or his college diplomas to show he earned a law degree. He changed his story to say that he had talked to a retired lawyer who told him what he needed to do. Adam also denied what he told Miki even though she had a written record of what he said. (She always had a pen and notepad with her to take notes as people said things.) Miki had seen firsthand what was currently happening in my dad's community and she knew what I'd told her was true because she witnessed similar events. Yet Adam now denied telling her anything. And he told me he did not want to talk about his life anymore. He said there are times when you just zip your mouth and not say anything. Well, that only happens when a person is doing something wrong or illegal. There is no reason to hide anything if you are perfectly legal or in the right. I would have no problem showing you my diploma from any school and I would show you my badge, without question, if I had one.

Something that bothered me was how Adam was Amish and claimed his church supported him. I struggled to understand how that was possible. As far back as I can remember, Amish people have never used law enforcement or the court system to defend themselves. I grew up Amish and lived in that culture for over forty years. I know the teachings and the ordnung (rules). And I didn't get all those teachings from my dad either. Over the years, I lived in several different church districts where my dad was not even involved with the leadership. The bishops of each district had the same rules all the others did. Not everyone listens and obeys the rules, which results in shunning, but all the Amish still know the rules. If I believed Adam's story and what he claimed, that meant the Amish had strayed from their own teachings and rules. Yet when I talked to others in the Amish community, they still teach and believe like they always have. I knew deception was happening.

I told Adam I couldn't imagine the Amish church I grew up in allowing him to do the things he does as an Amish person. And by Amish church, I don't mean the Bergholz community. Just the Amish church in general. Adam told me he just had to be very careful in what he said and what they didn't know wouldn't hurt them. He's absolutely right except in the end it is going to hurt Adam himself. He may not realize that just yet, but one day he will.

As you know, I'm no longer Amish. What happens among the Amish is not my concern, so I never planned to do anything about Adam's actions or what he said. However, when he used my own information against me and claimed to do things the Amish were not permitted to do, I decided otherwise. Eli, Miki, and I reported Adam and his actions to his church district leadership before the situation escalated and got out of hand. The bishops gave us the impression that they didn't know all the things Adam was doing.

Why do I tell you about Adam? Partly because it looks like my dad was right all those years ago about Adam being dishonest and doing wrong things. But also to show how two wrongs don't make a right. My dad did not have the right to manipulate the situation to try and beat Adam at life. My story illustrates how that manipulation affected all of us. And now both my dad and Adam are in the wrong.

Because Adam went after the wrong people, mainly me for doing the videos, my dad is getting away with his actions again. The girls in the Bergholz community wear scarves again, covering their shaggy haircuts. And the girls won't talk to outsiders anymore.

-28-

Final Thoughts

MY SIMPLE STORY IS JUST part of the uncovering of the Bergholz Amish Community. If you read *Betrayed and Rejected*, my first book, you know how all the events lead back to Adam and Winnie wanting to leave Bergholz. During the court case, my dad complained that the other Amish communities were not treating him fairly. Yet the other communities thought they won the whole case because Adam received custody of his girls and Bergholz people ended up in federal prison.

I remember back when my brother Elmer was possessed by the devil and said that our situation and story was going to be spread worldwide. Boy, was he ever right. He also asked Dad what he would do if both he and Adam were in the wrong. Elmer said, "Two wrongs don't make a right, and one right doesn't make two wrongs." At the time, I asked Elmer to apologize to Dad, but Elmer straight up told me there was no way he was apologizing for anything. Looking back, Elmer's words are how I know God was speaking.

In reality, neither my dad's community nor the other communities are exactly right. They are both in the wrong. Yet each community goes their own way thinking God is with them and not with others. How do I know neither are right? My dad has Winnie, who is divorced. Adam has full custody of his girls. If Dad were right, he would have Winnie and the girls. If Adam were right, he would have Winnie and the girls. Yet, each community has one part—Dad has Winnie and Adam has the girls.

My eyes are open in so many ways, and I can clearly see why God led me and my children out into the English world. I've tried my best to explain to the rest of the women in the Bergholz Amish that no matter what my dad teaches, the Bible stands firm and to listen to the Bible, not Dad's teachings. But Dad told everyone to put the Bible aside, just listen to him, and not question him.

I also told the women in plain words that the only way to stand with Dad is to lie about what he says. Sadly, some in the community, and my sister Winnie is one, believe it is okay to lie as long as you are living on God's path. I shake my head because I know where that path will lead. They have no idea where the devil is right now. Their minds are being manipulated, and they believe their own lies. Dad himself has said he doesn't know who they are because they're not Amish, not English, and not Mennonite. Unfortunately, I know who they are—hypocrites as demonstrated by their lives and actions. They wear clothes that look

Amish but are not. They do things the world does but while wearing Amish clothes and then lie about doing those things.

To this day, as I type this book, I am still the only woman from Bergholz who has escaped my dad's poisonous teachings. Sadly, the other women will never find the truth unless they have the opportunity to leave the Bergholz Amish community and join the Englishers. I read somewhere that it takes about two to four days to get someone out of the lies they've believed for so many years. The best way to get someone away from lies is to give testimonials and talk about both sides of the story. It clears their mind every time.

Epilogue

My life continues as usual outside the Amish community. While I never would've chosen the path that led me out, I am thankful I had the opportunity. The ones left behind in Bergholz now treat me and my children the exact same way that my dad claimed the other Amish communities treated him—they won't speak to us, and they avoid us.

Over the years, I've learned that the best way to help my dad is to back off and let God handle him. Dad refuses to listen to any of us and now says the people that left the community are traitors. I find that funny because we tried to tell him we didn't agree with what he was doing and that resulted in us leaving or being kicked out. Dad claims we are out here fighting him, but he's so far off from the Amish ways that the fight isn't worth fighting.

After my dad finished his prison sentence, he married Louisa. She is what he wanted the whole time. My cousin Ed had

Me and my eight children who left the Amish. Today, only two of my children, one son and one daughter, remain Amish.

never done anything wrong at all. My dad wanted his wife and was going to take her regardless. His actions made Ed look bad because my dad felt guilty. Everyone knows that if Dad hadn't used God's name, Louisa would have never left her husband and the father of her children. To this day, Dad's guilt eats him up because he keeps writing letters to others trying to make Ed look bad. Why pour all this bad talk on Ed when Dad is the one who manipulated Louisa?

After twenty-five years of living in Bergholz, both as Amish and English, I'm proud to say I moved away from the area. My Amish family members don't know where I live, and I hope to keep it that way. My life is good and peaceful.

Most of my eight boys who left the Amish with me are married or dating at this time. I have tried dating sites, but nothing came out of those yet. I think it's going to be better to wait on

God to send a man my way like he promised he would. Time will tell. My hope is that my two books will some day be made into a movie. And in the movie you will find out if I ever met that man of my dreams God promised me.

Not too long ago, Elias wrote me a lengthy letter, about six or seven pages, telling me how much he misses me and wants to marry me again. What he doesn't realize is that the woman he was married to for twenty-five years is dead. My life is changed, and I won't ever be the same again. I am saved now and have been born again into the kingdom of God.

Things don't always go the way we want them to, but God has a plan. My story is real, and I lived through it all—the joys, the trauma, the love, the heartaches. I just wish I could understand God and his ways better. To do that, my desire is to continue to follow him and watch and learn.

Written with much love and prayers for all my readers to find Jesus the way I found him.

Acknowledgments

WITHOUT THE HELP AND PRAYERS of many, I never would've been able to tell my story on my own.

To all my boys, thank you for sticking with me and for trusting me when we left the Amish. Some days weren't easy, but we survived together. And thank you for allowing me to include you in my story. I love you all!

To my pastor at Grace Point Ministry, thank you for standing with my family, supporting me, and helping me learn. It wasn't easy un-learning all the things I had been taught about God. Thank you for showing me the truth of who God is and what a real man of God is truly like.

To my editor, Kara Starcher of Mountain Creek Books, thank you for taking my words and making them a story. Writing down my story was hard, not just because it was emotional and I had to relive memories, but because I didn't understand how to write.

You took my attempts at chapters and made them into a story people want to read.

To my cover designer, Josh Aul of NexLevel Media, thank you for the beautiful book covers.

To Joe and Linda Fogle, thank you for all the work you did helping me modernize my Amish house and make it an English house with electric. And Linda, you're the one who changed the dozens of names in my books. Thank you for keeping track of those details.

And to those I've already mentioned in the pages of this book who supported me and encouraged me through the years, you know who you are and I thank you.

About the Author

Linda Shrock left the Amish of Bergholz, Ohio, in 2012 after leading a very dark, confusing life. She was married for twenty-seven years and has ten children. She was living a normal Amish life when some problems occurred and she ended up serving a two-year prison sentence in federal prison. Her time in prison changed her life completely. She was introduced to many other people and to church in prison where she found freedom and the Light of Jesus. She is now living a peaceful, quiet life in town with some of her children and attends Grace Point Ministry church. Through all her struggles, God has been so good to her.